My Girl

My Girl

STACE DON

WITH SUNDAY TIMES BESTSELLING AUTHOR
ANN CUSACK

MIRROR BOOKS

MIRROR BOOKS

1

Published in Great Britain and Ireland in 2025 by
Mirror Books, a Reach PLC business.

Photographic Acknowledgements: Alamy

www.mirrorbooks.co.uk
@TheMirrorBooks

Print ISBN 9781915306869
eBook ISBN 9781915306876

Editing and Production: Jo Sollis, Christine Costello
Cover Design: Jonah Webb

Printed and bound in Great Britain by
CPI Group (UK) Ltd, Croydon, CR0 4YY

To my daughter, who gives me strength every day to push forward. My fiancée for being my rock. And to every survivor out there. We are not victims we are warriors!

PROLOGUE

SUMMER 1996, STOCKPORT

FOR WEEKS now, I'd been looking longingly from my bedroom window at this pyramid of sand, imagining how much fun it would be racing up and down the slopes. But now that I was here, the reality was disappointingly different. With each step I sank further into the sand, right up to my knees, and I could hardly walk, never mind run. It didn't help that I was, as usual, wearing my football boots.

"Come on, Stace!" yelled my friend, Mandy, chucking a handful of sand in my direction.

I laughed and kicked a clod back at her, but not before sneaking a furtive glance over my shoulder, back at the house. At seven, I was expressly forbidden from coming to the park on my own. If Mum or Dad so much as walked past an upstairs window, they'd be sure to see me, perched on the sand, my disobedience flashing like a beacon right across the park.

My heart fell at the thought of letting them both down.

The fear of being a disappointment was far worse than any punishment, and suddenly this sandy mess was the last place I wanted to be.

"Mand, I'm off to play footie," I announced, sliding back down the mountain.

I knew my parents were far less likely to spot me down here, behind the trees. It wasn't even beach sand, I consoled myself. This coarse stuff was no good for sandcastles. Well, I decided, shaking out my football boots, I'd get some practice in, saving free kicks instead.

"You be Fowler, I'll be Schmeichel," I yelled, tearing off towards the rusty goal frame at the other side of the park. I threw the football high into the air for a header whilst I waited for Mand. But before it landed, I felt a tap on my shoulder.

"Hello Lou-Lou," said a strange male voice.

I spun around; stunned. The man had dark, spiky hair and cold, hard eyes, like two black marbles. Long, nicotine-stained hairs protruded from his nose and, revulsed, I shuddered a little. I didn't recognise him at all. Yet Lou was my middle name. How did he know that? My first thought was maybe Mum and Dad had secretly enlisted this man to apprehend me in the park, a sort of privately hired policeman, if there was such a thing.

"Do you know who I am?" he asked.

I grabbed my ball under my arm and studied my boots. I felt silly explaining my policeman theory out loud. Besides, he radiated something sinister. Those eyes. Those nose hairs. I had been told never to talk to strangers and I suddenly thought perhaps this was one of the bad men I'd learned about in school. Again, that menacing feeling crept like cold fingers around my collar.

"Do you?" he pressed.

Stubbornly, I stared at my boots. I had sand in my footie socks, rubbing between my toes, and I hoped Mum wouldn't notice. I hoped she wasn't looking out of the window, right now. The minutes seemed to elongate and stretch between us, and it felt like such a long time until he spoke again.

"Well, Lou-Lou," he said. "I'm your dad."

There was a whoosh, like a breaking wave, in my ears, and instantly time was racing, speeding, hurtling past me.

"You're not," I stuttered, forgetting the rule about talking to strangers. "You are not! My dad is at home and he's waiting for me."

A terrifying thought crashed through my mind. What if something awful had happened to my dad, and this man had come to replace him? I set off running, blood pounding like a marching army in my ears, tears streaming down my cheeks, the studs of my boots clattering along the path. Banging on the front door, I fell into the hallway and collapsed, sobbing, in a heap.

"There's a scary man in the park who says he's my dad," I cried. "And he's not, is he?"

Too late, I realised, I'd dropped myself right in it. I'd admitted being in the park. But to my relief – and then my unease – nobody even noticed. There was an eerie silence which was a thousand times worse than being told off. Fear bloomed in my chest. Wordlessly, Dad picked me up off the carpet and carried me into the living room. I wanted the sort of explanation that keeps a child happy, ties up all the loose ends, shuts off further questions.

Oh, don't you worry about him, he's a liar. The police will be arresting him later. Forget about him now and have your tea. Cheesy pizza tonight.

Instead, he sighed heavily and turned to my mother. When he finally spoke, his voice was quiet and solemn, each word loaded with significance.

"I think we should call the social worker," he said. "Stace needs to know."

HURTLING DOWN the stairs, bursting with the excitement of a freshly hatched seven-year-old, I couldn't wait to open my presents.

"Happy Birthday, sweet pea," called my mother, Claire, from the kitchen. "Your breakfast is ready, though I've a feeling it might have to wait!"

I pushed open the living room door and gasped, for in the middle of the floor there was an extravagant pile of gifts, all for me.

"Which one first?" grinned my father, Pete, pulling me in for a hug. "I can't believe our baby girl is seven years old."

I was, as usual, spoiled to bits. There were sweets, toys and clothes. But my favourite presents were, without contest, a new football, a pair of goalie gloves and a yellow Liverpool football kit, including a goalie shirt. All thoughts of breakfast forgotten, I pulled the shirt on over my pyjamas and ran out into the back garden with my ball under my arm.

"Penalty kicks!" I yelled, standing in goal. "Who's going first?"

My older brothers, Daniel and Paul, and sister, Donna, dutifully trailed outside, still bleary-eyed and in their dressing gowns, to take a birthday penalty. All in their late teens, nothing was ever too much trouble for their baby sister. I was the youngest in the family, and I was coddled and cosseted like a guest of honour in my own home. My life was neatly and beautifully choreographed at every turn. Daniel, the eldest, was a Liverpool fan, and had bought me the footie kit, as a way of bribing me to support his team, because I was a Manchester United supporter.

"We can get matching kits, and watch the games together," he suggested.

"Okay," I agreed readily.

I loved football, pure and simple, regardless of the teams. At school, I played striker for the team – the only girl out of 11 players – and I scored in most games. Each evening, I was out in the back garden or in the street with my pals and a football. And when I wasn't playing football, I was watching it. We had Sky TV, especially so I could follow every game. And even then, it wasn't enough. On Saturday mornings, I'd tune into highlights from the Italian league. I couldn't understand a word they were saying, but that didn't matter. I had Subbuteo, a table football game, and I collected football stickers too. In the same way other children got sweets as a treat, I'd get a packet of stickers. My pocket money was usually divided between Thorntons chocolate footballs, and my beloved stickers. My sticker book, as holy as a bible, was home to such greats as Robbie Fowler, Ole Solskjaer, Nicky Butt and Fabrizio Ravanelli. Every player was assigned scores for passing, shooting, tackling and running, and I soaked up the statistics like a sponge. I knew them all off by heart. Each week, I wrote down all the scores from every match and I cast a critical eye over each tackle and each goal. Later I recreated the best ones in my own back garden. So for me, my yellow Liverpool kit, regardless of the team, was my favourite gift.

I looked up to my big brother, just as I did my footballing idols. And so I was more than happy to take the bribe. After a birthday tea with my friends, I puffed up my cheeks to blow out the candles on my chocolate caterpillar cake.

"Make a wish," Mum instructed.

I closed my eyes and screwed up my face, but in truth, I could think of nothing I needed or wanted. My life was just about perfect. Standing here in my dining room, surrounded by a nucleus of loving and much-loved faces, I was filled to the brim with happiness, right from the top of my light-brown ponytail to the tips of my black Diadora football boots.

"I wish that nothing changes, ever," I whispered to myself, and then one by one, the seven candles were snuffed out.

1

BORN IN April 1989, I lived in Stockport, Cheshire, with my parents and my three older siblings. We also had a dog, Benny, two cats, Sooty and Sweep, a hamster and a goldfish.

Our home, on a small estate, was on a quiet road overlooking a park, and overrun with kids my age. I was friends with everyone – in that way that children are – and there was always enough of us for two teams, a full subs bench and a referee.

Downstairs, separate from our living room and dining room, I had my very own playroom, overflowing with toys. Though I was a tomboy at heart, I had a girly side, and I loved playing with Polly Pocket and Barbie dolls. I was an avid reader too, and the shelves were lined with Terry Pratchett and Roald Dahl books, though there were plenty of football autobiographies mixed in. My David Beckham and Eric Cantona books were sacred, and they were neatly stacked in pride of place on a shelf above my bed.

There were three bedrooms, the boys shared one, Donna and I had another, our parents had the third. Even though

Donna was 16, nearly 10 years older than me, we were best pals. In my top bunk, I'd lie back and listen as she read me chapters from Fantastic Mr Fox and James and the Giant Peach. We'd have play-fights, her pinning me down and tickling me on our parents' bed.

"Death by tickling! No mercy!" she yelled, and it just made me laugh all the more. She always let me win, in the end.

Mum, small and plump with a neat bob, worked in the office at my primary school. I arrived with her each morning, waiting in the office until it was time for the bell, and I almost felt like part of the staff as I greeted the teachers and cleaners and caretakers. I'd hear the teachers call each other by their first names and moan about their hangovers, and I felt so lucky; I was being treated to private snippets the other children did not see and I embraced my secrets with glee. Here, as at home, I was so fortunate, and I knew it. During the school day, I was always the one called upon to run errands, a message for the headteacher or perhaps a package for the office.

"Send Mrs Robinson's daughter," the teachers would say, with a trusting nod of approval. "She's a sensible girl."

Aged seven, I puffed up with importance, like a small bird preening her wings. I loved the responsibility and the knowledge that I was needed and valued. School was, in many ways, simply a comfortable extension of my home life.

In class, I worked hard, and my behaviour was impeccable. As Mrs Robinson's daughter, I had a lot to live up to, after all. In addition to football, I played chess and violin, and I had lessons in Irish dancing. Mum never missed a single match or performance; she was there on the touchline, cheering me on, or she'd be sitting in the audience, clapping my violin solo or my dance routines. If Dad wasn't working, he came down to watch my matches, too.

"Brilliant goal Stace!" he yelled, clapping his hands high in the air. "Brilliant!"

He was not a particularly avid football fan, but in his eyes, I could do no wrong. I could have scored an own-goal, and he'd have been just as pleased. Having such belief, such love, behind me, was a little like a jet engine powering me through life.

At home, my parents had defined roles. Typical of a school secretary, Mum was organised, straight-forward, and could be strict at times. But she also had an abundance of patience. From being small, I'd been a fussy eater, and after starting school, my eating issues became less of a choice and more of an illness. I'd no idea why, but certain smells and specific textures would make me retch. Mum tried all sorts of combinations until one day, after I spotted a jar of beetroot on the dining table, I vomited all over my roast dinner. Conceding another approach was needed, she tried me with a single food group at a time. One afternoon, I was presented with a plate of plain roast chicken. I could not face the idea of putting it in my mouth, but neither could I bear to let her down. Luckily, I was wearing my favourite denim skirt, with pockets on each side, and I spent the entire meal chewing on thin air whilst stuffing bits of chicken into my pockets.

"All finished!" I announced when the last slice was safely hidden away.

But Mum was not fooled.

"Empty your pockets please," she said, suppressing a smile. "I don't mind that you didn't eat your dinner Stace, but I don't like you telling lies. You understand that, don't you?"

I nodded miserably. I hated being in trouble. But after what we always referred to as the denim-skirt incident, Mum devised a menu just for me, a different dish every night: cheese pizza, scrambled egg, jacket potato, turkey dinosaurs, egg and chips, waffles and nuggets. The weekly menu was written out and fixed onto the door of the fridge with a magnet, so I had advance warning of every meal. Within this scaffold of routine, I felt comfortable and safe. It was reassuring to know exactly which meal awaited me on which day. Donna taught me how to make scrambled eggs, and, as I stirred the pan under her watchful eye, she was full of advice and compliments.

"They look perfect," she told me. "Ready to serve. You've done a good job there, Stace."

Nobody made me feel out of place or awkward, so much so that my irregular eating habits ironically became the norm. Only years later would I understand the shocking reason for my disorder, but back then, picking at my turkey dinosaurs, I was quite content.

Mum was in charge of discipline too. I was polite and well-behaved but, at the first sign of a punishment, I'd race upstairs and climb into my wardrobe, hiding behind my Manchester United shirts. For some reason I thought that if I disappeared, the problem would disappear with me. Mum's idea of punishment was usually a stern telling off, but it was mortifying for me simply to know I had upset her. Being a disappointment to my parents was the worst feeling. Once, after a minor fall-out with a friend who was calling me mean names, I refused to let her join in my game of elastics outside our house.

"Come here, right now!" Mum called from the front doorstep. "You play nicely, Stace, or not at all. Say sorry this instant!"

Burning with humiliation, I ran right past her, up to my bedroom, and clambered into the wardrobe, which was tall and wooden with patterned panels and folding doors. I felt like I'd been huddled up in there for ages when I heard the familiar tune of the ice-cream van in the street.

Suddenly, I was faced with a dilemma. I was always, always, allowed to buy an ice-cream. But how to get over my sulk? Visualising a 99 with sprinkles, I crept downstairs. Mum had left 50p by the front door, as usual, ready for my ice cream. But as my hand stretched out to claim it, she called, "Say sorry Stace, or there is no ice-cream."

"Sorry," I said, in a small voice, and I was, truly.

I got my ice cream, and I got a good talking to in the bargain.

"You can't keep hiding in that wardrobe," Mum said. "You're old enough to stay and face the music now."

But I loved my place as the baby of the family, cocooned with love, and we both knew there was little chance of me growing up any time soon. Dad complemented Mum perfectly. He often worked late, and when he got home, he was all about affection and fun.

"Where's my special girl?" he'd shout, waiting for me to jump into his arms.

He was always ready with a cuddle, and I'd sit on his knee for hours whilst he played card games on his computer. On Saturday mornings, he listened, with a straight face, to me practising my recorder and violin. It is fair to say I was not as musical as I was sporty, but he sat and clapped my performances regardless. Other weekends, we'd go around car boot sales, picking out bargains, little toys or quirky finds. Once, he bought me a whole box of McDonald's wind-up toys, and I was thrilled. On our way home, Dad might stop at the bookies and put a pound each way on his chosen horse.

"Our little secret, Stace," he said, tapping the side of his nose, and I laughed and tapped mine in return.

We both knew Mum wouldn't approve of him gambling, even if it was just a bit of fun. I loved those car boot trips and loved that we had a secret. These were little scraps sewn together to produce the rich fabric which made up our happy family life.

Every Sunday morning, we went to church. Unlike many kids, I enjoyed going to church, standing with my family and singing hymns at the top of my lungs. I hoped to be allowed to train as an altar girl when I was old enough. Around once a month, I went to confession, where I was handed a penance, in the form of prayers, which had to be recited silently before I was allowed to leave the church. Depending on the severity of the sins, penance could be one prayer, or it could be 50. Coming out of confession, I focussed on timing how long everyone else was praying for; if there were people with a long penance, it was a safe bet they had a long list of sins. I'd usually forgotten my own penance completely in my eagerness to guess what everyone else had done wrong.

"Stace!" my mother hissed, under her breath. "Bow your head and say your penance."

For my first communion, I got a new white dress with a veil and white shoes. My parents bought me a pink candle, which I still have to this day, and a Bible, which was inscribed: *To Stace, love Mum and Dad.*

For my confirmation, I was required to choose a name, which would be added to my own. I was supposed to select the name of a saint who was especially inspiring to me, but instead I just picked out the longest name I could find: 'Bernadette', as compensation for my own name which I believed was woefully short.

"Stace Louise Bernadette," I beamed. "I like the sound of it."

In the summer holidays, we'd spend time at our caravan in Scarborough. Even if we were only going away overnight, I packed my Beckham and Cantona books religiously. I never went anywhere without them.

"You'd rather forget your clothes than those football books," Dad joked as he loaded up the car.

Our caravan was near a funfair and the beach – and best of all, there were acres of green fields where I could play. But as long as I had my football, I was happy anywhere. I'd pull on a pair of joggers and a hoodie, and I'd play out all day, regardless of the weather. Mostly it was rain, but it never bothered me. In my heart, there was plenty of sunshine.

Mine were not the sort of parents to force me into wearing a scratchy dress. I even attended Irish Dancing class in my tracksuit top and joggers so that I could quickly rush outside to play football the moment it was over. Mum and Dad embraced who I was completely.

Also in the holidays, I'd have sleepovers at my paternal gran's, who seemed ancient to me, and yet loved to bop around her kitchen to the latest hits on the radio. She still went to the market twice a week for her shopping too. She was small and skinny with white bouffant hair piled on her head like a whippy ice cream. Even as a child, I was almost as tall as she was. On her worktop, she had a big biscuit barrel, and my first job was usually to drag a pouffe from the lounge into the kitchen to reach a biscuit for us both. Then she'd pull me onto her knee and tell me about the war years. She showed me an old ration book and I was transfixed by her stories, fascinated by tales of years gone by. She and I slept in the same double bed, and I loved warming my feet on her soft winceyette nightdress. One summer, Gran took me on holiday to Blackpool and on the beach, whilst other kids paddled or built sandcastles, I practised keepy-ups with my football. My love of the sport ran right through me, like a stick of Blackpool rock.

"Oh Stace, you're glued to that football," Gran chuckled.

Occasionally, we'd visit my maternal grandparents for Sunday lunch. Even though we didn't see them often, they knew all about my safe foods, and my plate of mash and gravy was served without question. Everyone made allowances around me, and everyone made sure I was okay. I appreciated it in so far as it was all I had ever known. Ours was a close family, and a tight-knit community, and our neighbours and friends were often in and out of the house. We had social workers visiting too, which I didn't once question. I thought everyone had a social worker. Or perhaps, I told myself, it was connected with Mum's job at the school. So, when the social worker sat at the dining table with me, completing activity packs and asking questions about my week at school, I thought it was all perfectly standard. I never challenged it because I just was not that sort of child. My only worries were all centred on the football field.

"Now, you be a good girl for your Mummy," the social worker said, as she was leaving.

And if there was an emphasis on *Mummy*, then I did not hear it. Perhaps I chose not to. If she was awkward, or overly deliberate, I did not notice. I was blissfully oblivious. I had no sense whatsoever that everyone around me knew something I did not.

2

BUT THEN came the trip to the park on the sand pyramid. For so long afterwards, I blamed myself. I was, after all, forbidden from going to the park alone. If only I'd done as I was told, if only I'd followed instructions, I would never have bumped into him. Never bumped into the scary man with the cold eyes and nose hairs who claimed to be my father. It was all my fault. That night, after the park, Mum packed me off to bed early, without my usual bedtime story. But with the bedroom door open, I heard her and Dad talking in low, urgent voices.

"Double check the windows, I'll lock the back door and the gate as well."

"We need to call social services, first thing."

A sickly dread seeped through me as, even from my bedroom, I felt the bristle of quiet panic. I was usually a good sleeper but that night I lay awake, long after Donna had drifted off. There was no possible way that man could be my father. No way. My dad was fast asleep, in the next bedroom. In fact, I could hear him snoring lightly and soothingly through the walls. That man was, I decided, most likely a baddie. I'd stayed awake the previous weekend while Donna watched a documentary in bed about a paedophile with ginger hair who had snatched a child from the street. She'd thought I was asleep, but instead I'd been watching her scary programme through screwed up eyes. The idea that I'd been so close to a real-life criminal was petrifying. It certainly explained why Mum and Dad were so afraid. And yet, as I dozed off, something poked at me, like a finger jabbing at my arm. Something wasn't quite right. Because if he was a total stranger, how on earth did he know my middle name?

Well, Lou-Lou, I'm your dad.

The next morning, Mum informed me I would not be allowed out to play for a whole week. Though the sanction was a blow, it was also kind of reassuring; this was the reaction I would and should have expected for my disobedience in going to the park. Life, perhaps, was slotting gratefully back into the normal channels. But then, she said, "The social worker will be coming to see us after school. We need to talk to you."

Her words squatted, undigested, in my stomach all day. There was a gnawing, dragging, fear. I didn't want to hear what they had to say and yet I didn't know why. That evening, two social workers showed up, one man, one woman. I was ushered into the living room alongside them, and to my surprise, Mum waited outside.

"Stace there is something you need to understand," said the female social worker. "Your mum, who you live here with, is not your real mum. She's not your birth mum."

This threw me completely. I had been expecting them to address the issue of the kidnapper in the park. What on earth did this have to do with my mother? There was a silence which stabbed at my heart, and she said again, gently, "Claire Robinson is not your mother."

"That's not true," I said in a low, fierce voice, kicking the sofa hard with the backs of my heels. "That isn't right."

"It is, Stace. Pete and Claire are your foster parents. You came to live here when you were a baby. They are not your real parents. This is why we did the life story book with you. I'm sorry, I know this is a lot to take in. Would you like to ask any questions?"

This was the male social worker talking now. From nowhere, I was ablaze with fury. I stood up smartly and marched out of the room without replying.

I had never felt so angry in my entire life. In the hallway, the ground seemed to move beneath me. I clutched onto the banister, as my world tipped and pitched, like a small boat in a storm. Around me, on the walls, the fireplaces, the tables, were photos of me. The house was like a shrine. I had never given these pictures much thought; this was simply affirmation that I was cherished and adored. But now, as I peered at each snapshot, I realised there was not a single baby photo. Not one. They started of me as a toddler and went upwards. My older siblings were on certain photos, and there was a resemblance running through them, same nose, similar colouring, same smile. What about me; the ugly duckling? Why didn't I look like them too? It had never even occurred to me, until now. And why were they all so much older than

I was? There was over nine years between Donna and I, and my brothers were even older than her. I had a different surname too; they were all Robinson, yet my last name was Taylor. Why had I never questioned that?

Perhaps, deep down, I just didn't want to know. I was happy in my own little protected bubble, and I looked no further than my family and my football; I needed nothing else. Yet, as the facts slowly descended on me, like a toxic smog, I felt sickened. It was all slotting into place like the world's worst jigsaw.

Your mum, who you live here with, is not your real mum.

Shellshocked, I crawled upstairs and into my bedroom. Sobbing, I lay on my bunk, staring at my belongings. My favourite Polly Pocket was perched on the edge of my shelf next to my football books, and a small clay house which I had made at school and was immensely proud of. My rosettes and certificates hung on the wall around my bed, each with a precious memory attached. On the opposite wall, I had posters of Robbie Fowler, Eric Cantona and of course, David Beckham. I had a new Liverpool FC duvet, to go with my new footie kit, but I also had a Manchester United duvet in the laundry. These were all the things that made me who I was. Or so I'd thought.

But who was I?

Who was I really?

I had no memories of another family, of other parents, of any life other than this one. Nothing. There had not been a single clue that I did not belong here, or if there was, I had missed it. Perhaps I had subconsciously ignored it. The door opened a little, and Mum popped her head around the gap.

"Baked potato? I've scooped it out and mashed it up, just how you like it," she said. "Come on, love, you need to eat."

"No," I choked out, and buried my face in my pillow.

A little while later, Donna came in.

"Come on Stace," she said gently. "I'll wrestle you. Tickle you to death. Do you fancy it?"

Again, I was lit up with rage, surging through me like a thousand volts. How dare she use that phrase? I played wrestling with my big sister. Not her.

"No," I said, my teeth gritted.

She must have known. They must all have known. Everyone except me. Her life was real, and mine wasn't, and in that moment, I hated her for it.

3

ALL THAT week, I was in a daze. There was no mention or reference to what had happened, save for Mum reminding me that I was grounded.

"You can't go out for the rest of the week," she told me. "You'll have to play in the back garden."

But nobody spoke about the man in the park. No one talked about the social worker and the bombshell she had dropped in my lap. Yet everywhere, the house felt different. The air was heavy and polluted. Our house was usually open and friendly but as I mooched around, each door seemed to shut in my face. There were no answers, no reassurances. Only closed doors and dead ends.

I have spent much of my adult life looking back on this time, wondering why my foster parents did not address the issue with me and why they had let the situation take shape at all. Why was I raised, believing I was their birth child? As I got older, I was assured that my social workers had tried to explain my complex family situation to me. I do remember doing scrapbooks and sticking in photos and mementos.

Perhaps I wasn't listening. Perhaps I didn't want to listen. And maybe my foster parents, as time went on, simply took the easiest option, and followed my lead. Perhaps they, like me, wanted to believe that I was theirs. Sieving my childhood memories through an adult filter, I can see only a small and frightened child, who no longer belonged. After the social workers came, perhaps they were told not to discuss my birth parents with me. It might be that they were too upset, or afraid. But I was just seven years old. I, too, was upset and afraid. And I felt so alone.

At the end of the week, I was finally allowed to play out again. My feet were itching to kick a football out on the front with my mates. I'd been playing on my own, in the back garden, every evening, which wasn't so much fun.

"Remember Stace, stay away from the park," Mum told me. "You know the rules."

I didn't reply. Instead, I remembered her making me empty out the scraps of chicken from my denim skirt pockets.

I don't like you telling lies. You understand that don't you?

Yet everyone had lied to me. Over and over again. That was certainly how it seemed to me. I thought I had two brothers and a sister. I thought I had a mum and dad. It was all a sham, a façade, a pretence. I had been brought up never to tell lies and yet my whole life was a lie. One rule for them, and another for me.

The paradox of my safe and solid existence, now unveiled as a tumbling house of cards, was as cruel as it was shocking. Again, I was consumed with rage so intense that I was trembling as I closed the front door behind me.

Without caring who saw me, without even bothering to take a diversion, I walked straight into the park. So what if 'Mum' and 'Dad' caught me? What was it to them? A sixth sense told me the man would be there, and, as I rounded the corner, I was right. My stomach churned with a cocktail of fear, curiosity and excitement. But as I got closer, and I saw his hard-pebble eyes, my resolve cracked. I wanted to turn and run, but it was too late.

"I've been watching you," he said.

I did not speak. But in the depths of my mind, a warning bell clanged. I didn't know this man, yet already he was controlling and manipulating me. As a seven-year-old, it translated as pure terror.

"I've been watching you," he repeated. "I know you've not been allowed to play out. Is that because of me?"

Again, I did not, could not, speak.

"Come back tomorrow," he said eventually. "I'll buy you some sweets. I'm your dad, Lou-Lou. Remember that."

I did not want to see him. He unsettled me. Frightened me. His eyes seemed to drill into me. And yet the next day after school, my legs carried me into the park, as though I had no control over them. Through my confusion, I realised I was here in the park primarily to hurt my parents. I wanted to make them sad, just like I was sad. Those first few meetings with the man were about rebellion and revenge, and nothing else.

"I'll get you the sweets, like I promised," he said. "I keep my promises. See?"

Again, I did not speak but something soured within me.

The man took me to the corner shop, and though I was quaking at the thought of being spotted or challenged, either by my own family or a neighbour, I walked in with my head up. The anger was still there, sizzling and hissing, like a disgruntled snake under my skin.

"What would you like?" he asked, sweeping his hand across the jars of sweets. Wordlessly, I pointed to the strawberry bon bons. I knew it was rude not to say thank you, but I could not find my voice.

I went home, without having spoken. But all night, his words rang in my ears, and I realised he was right. He had kept his promise. My own parents, however, had not.

The next day, I had a football match after school, and Mum and Dad both came to cheer me on. Playing football was, in many ways, a wonderful release, my only chance to empty my mind of the fury and worry which had swirled since the social workers' visit. But deep down was the suspicion that this, too, was a sham. Who were these people, shouting my name, celebrating my goal? They were not my parents. They were nothing to do with me. And again, I felt a panic which notched up into an angry growl, swelling and gurgling in my throat.

"Well played, Stace," Dad called, as the full-time whistle blew.

I wanted so much to run over to him, to feel his strong arms lift me off the floor. But instead, I skulked back to the changing rooms on my own. The day after, I slipped out to the park, and the man was there, this time with a handful of photos. Despite myself, I could not help being inquisitive.

"Here's you as a baby," he said. "Another one of you with your Mum. Oh, and here's my favourite, you and me, Stace. Dad and daughter."

I stared. I sort of recognised myself, on the toddler photos. Same brown eyes. In fact, as I peered closer, I realised I had the same colour eyes as the man. We shared the same chin too. I was both pleased and repulsed at the likeness. But no matter how much I tried; I had no memory of these photos. None at all.

"Here," he said. "You take these photos. Put them up in your bedroom."

Without speaking, I took them and stuffed them into my pocket.

See what they make of that," he smirked. "I wrote you lots of letters as well, bet you never got them, eh? I bought you loads of presents, Lou-Lou, every birthday, every Christmas. I love you so much. I've never forgotten you. I always know what you're up to and where you are. Remember that."

My eyes were wide with astonishment.

"Tell the social workers to show you the letters," he said, as he turned to leave. "They prove I'm telling the truth."

* * * *

Back at home, on my bed, I inspected the photos. More and more, I accepted I did look like that baby and there were definite similarities between myself and the man. With a flash of defiance, I climbed down from my bunk and pinned the photos around the frame of my bedroom mirror.

"There, see what they think of that," I told myself, realising I was repeating what the man had said to me.

Maybe he wasn't so bad after all. He'd bought me sweets. He'd shown me photos. Though it hadn't been spelled out to me, this man was clearly my father. He was the only one telling me the truth. Everyone else had lied to me and let me down. Maybe he was the only one I could really trust. When Mum saw the photos later that evening, her face crumpled with a frown.

"Please, Stace, we don't want you to see that man," she said. "You don't know what he's like. Please."

She was almost in tears, but for once, her distress did not touch me. A plaque hardened around my heart and suddenly being a disappointment to her was no longer the big deal it once was.

I was again grounded for a week, and this time, I sulked in my wardrobe, refusing to apologise. When the week was up, I went straight back to the park. It did not strike me as odd, sinister even, that the man seemed somehow to know my routine and watch my every move.

"Stace," he said, as I walked onto the grass. "You've been missing for a week. Where've you been?"

His tone was confrontational, not friendly. He was demanding an explanation. A shiver of unease rippled over my skin, but I said nothing.

"How come you support Liverpool?" he asked, nodding at my shirt. "I'm a United fan. I thought you were too."

Something shifted inside me. I was, after all, a Manchester United fan at heart and this was another link between us.

But still, I did not speak. When I got home, there was a social worker waiting.

"Your birth mother would like to see you," she told me. "We've made arrangements for you to visit this weekend, just for a couple of hours. Does that sound okay?"

Fidgeting, I screwed up my face. One minute, I was afraid. The next, upset. But overlaying all these emotions, was raw outrage. My life, as I knew it, did not exist. What did I have to lose?

"Yes," I said, in a clipped voice. "I'll go."

I turned to leave the room, but the social worker wasn't done with me yet.

"And about your dad," she said. "There are good reasons why it's not a good idea for you meet Nigel Taylor in the park. Can you please agree to stop seeing him?"

I felt my blood boiling. This was the first confirmation that the man was actually my dad. Everyone so far had stepped around the issue, like a dirty puddle. For the first time, I understood where my surname came from. He and I were both Taylor. I hated him for it, blamed him that I could not be Robinson like my siblings and my parents.

"Stace?" she pressed. "Do we have a deal? Will you stop meeting him?"

I bristled. It was him arranging the meetings, not me. Truth was, I didn't like seeing him. I only met him because I knew it would upset my parents; it was my only way of fighting back, of showing them how much I was hurting. I didn't know what else to do with the sadness inside me.

For the rest of the week, I was not allowed to play out at all.

"Grounded," I announced when my pals knocked on the door. "Can't come out. Sorry."

Normally, I'd have been wounded, watching them all play on the grass, whilst I was stuck inside. But I was also beginning to feel a sense of separation from them. Their lives had not changed. They had parents, siblings and relatives. I no longer belonged in their lives, just as they did not belong in mine. The disconnect felt like an open wound. Their parents, I worked out, must have known I was fostered. Perhaps my friends knew, too, and had been sworn to secrecy.

Maybe the whole world was in on the joke, and I was the last to know!

Lying on my bed, listening to my friends scream and laugh outside, I felt so lonely. I didn't know who my real parents were, or why I'd been taken away from them. Worst of all, I didn't know if I might be sent back. There were so many questions whirling like a snowstorm in my skull, but I didn't want the answers. I just wanted all of this to go away.

The next day, as I played five-a-side in the schoolyard at lunchtime, I spotted familiar-looking spiky hair above the railings and my heart lurched. It was him. I knew it was. Sure enough, his face appeared moments later, his eyes cold and hard, even from across the playground.

"Lou-Lou!" he called.

I froze. I didn't know what to do. Too scared to reply, too scared to run away. So I did nothing. I stood there, motionless, until he must have got annoyed, or been disturbed, and he walked away. That afternoon, as soon as I got home, I climbed straight into my wardrobe and hid myself right at the back, behind all my football shirts.

"Stace, come down, your pizza is ready," Mum called.

"No," I replied angrily. "I'm not moving."

I was so overwhelmed by feelings of rejection and hurt that rage was my only outlet. Deep down, I was scared, not angry. But back then, I didn't understand where all my fury was coming from. The anger was no more than a flimsy defence against the arrows the world was throwing at me. And my wardrobe was the only place I felt safe.

In total, in those early weeks, I saw my father seven times, either in the park, at the top of our street, or walking past my schoolyard. And then, on the eighth occasion, as I was on my way to my pal's, he materialised from behind a car, almost like a magic trick. I didn't know whether to be impressed or disturbed and, perhaps, I was a little of both.

"I'm going to court," he told me. "I'm going to make them let me see you. Just wait and see."

And with that, he vanished. The second part of the trick.

I ran home, again seeking refuge in my wardrobe. Burying my face in my David Beckham shirt, my whole body shook with sobs. I felt as though I'd fallen into someone else's life by mistake, and I desperately wanted to have mine back again.

4

IT WAS a bright Sunday morning when my mother announced she would drive me from our home in Stockport to my birth mother's home in Oldham. Now the day was here, I was not sure about going. Not sure at all.

"It will only be for an hour or two," she said. "Don't worry, Stace."

But how could I not? Mum and I were both quiet in the car, our anxieties bouncing between each other and back again, making us feel even worse. And when we arrived, outside the small semi-detached house, my panic suddenly shot up to the next level.

Outside, prowling the small garden, was a furious-looking pit bull terrier. I had thought my own anger was frightening, but this animal was a monster.

"I'm not getting out of the car," I said, gripping onto the handle. "I can't."

Although we had our own at home, I was generally wary of dogs. As I stepped onto the pavement, with Mum's encouragement, my fear of the dog and the visit itself merged and intensified. I barely noticed the young woman at the door, who guided the pit bull into the house before coming back to greet me.

"Hi," she said shyly. "I'm your mu – I'm Lisa."

By now, I was in tears. I could not even reply.

"The dog is in the back garden," she said. "Don't worry about him. He's not as scary as he looks."

But I did worry. I was worried about everything. And when Mum left, promising to pick me up later, I sobbed in despair. One minute, I was a carefree little girl who worried about nothing more than an off-side goal. The next, I became a neurotic kid, riddled with doubt and angst.

Inside the living room were three or four adults, more strange faces, and I felt even more overwhelmed. I spent most of the visit crying in the kitchen. Lisa was unsettlingly quiet. For a time, she sat at the dining table, but she seemed uneasy with me, and quickly wandered off. When she returned, she heated something on the stove, before presenting me with a plate of ravioli on toast. The smell alone was enough to make me gag, but I knew, through good manners, I had to at least try and eat a few mouthfuls. The squishy parcels felt like soft flesh between my teeth, and I retched each time I swallowed.

"I'm sorry," I mumbled eventually. "I'm just not very hungry."

It was a relief when Mum arrived to collect me, but to my dismay, I heard them making arrangements for me to return a couple of weeks later.

"Do I have to go?" I whined.

"It's not up to me," Mum replied. "We have to do as the social worker tells us."

Again, a swell of outrage. She was supposed to be my mother! Why wouldn't she help? My entire life had tumbled into a sink hole and there was nobody there to winch me out. As the days passed, my anger cooled into a cold defiance, and I decided that yes, I would show them. I would visit Lisa and I would make sure I enjoyed myself. Then they'd be sorry.

The second time, Mum drove me to a different address. Lisa had moved house, she explained. It wasn't far away, another neat semi, and the dreaded pit bull was already stowed away in the back garden. But the low-level anxiety lurked, always, in the back of my mind. What if he gets out? What if he bites? What if he eats me whole?

Lisa tried to be welcoming, but she was, again, very quiet and timid. Looking back the situation was probably almost as difficult for her as it was for me. We were two strangers, neither of us capable, nor even willing, to plant those first seeds needed to grow a relationship. She barely spoke and did not make eye contact. As last time, there were visitors, a boyfriend and a couple of his friends. They took little notice of me, but I found them intimidating. They were on one side, I was on another. All of them, against me.

"Do you want to go the shop, for sweets?" Lisa asked me.

I nodded readily, anxious to escape the chaos of the house. But my heart dropped when her boyfriend, Karl Brompton, decided to join us. Lisa barely spoke until we got to the shop.

"Choose whatever you like," she smiled.

I sensed she was trying to be friendly. She wanted to

welcome me. But she did not know how. Her home was nice, it was clean and tidy. There were a few toys, too. I had no issue with the place, except that it wasn't mine. I already had a home. Why would I want another?

* * * *

The visits continued, every other weekend, and I looked forward to them only in as much as I thought it was a way of wounding my parents. I took a football and played out in the street, mostly on my own. The back garden was out of bounds because of the dog. One afternoon, Lisa showed me a bedroom, unfurnished except for an unmade bed and a portable TV.

"If you like, you could sleep over next time," she said.

I shrugged awkwardly, not wanting to be rude. As I walked back onto the landing, Karl was waiting.

"You know, you should really be living here," he hissed. "Lisa is your mum. You belong with her, not with them."

I was winded by his words. I was being told, time and time again, that this woman was my mother. But because I could and would not accept it, I had instead buried it. I looked on Lisa as more of a distant relative, or a family friend. I couldn't see any resemblance between us, but nor was I looking for any. We both had long brown hair. We were both small and slight. But I didn't want to see the similarities. The dots were there but I refused to join them. And I hadn't equated the word mother with the role itself. Moreover, I had not for a moment thought she might try to replace or usurp my own mother. I had not considered it might have to be one or the other. Karl continued to glare and there was only one reply.

"Okay," I stuttered. "Okay. I'd like to stay overnight. Thank you."

And so, the next stage began. I did not think about where this might lead, and what the final aim might be. I lived, like most children, from one day to the next – I worried about football and little else. And staying overnight, I at least had a bedroom of my own, where I could retreat away from the noise. Lisa's house seemed always to be filled with other people. At home, I had a routine, I had discipline, I had order. Here, I could have spent the day in my room, and nobody would even notice. Left to my own devices, I realised I didn't like it.

The biggest downside to sleeping over at Lisa's was the mealtimes. I knew Mum had spoken with her about my eating issues because I'd heard the conversation. But it appeared that Lisa hadn't. And usually, the menu was not her decision anyway. Karl, or one of his friends, Ray or Deano, did the cooking.

"There," Ray said, slapping fish fingers and beans in front of me. "Eat up."

Briefly, I closed my eyes, wondering if I could somehow magic them away. I didn't eat fish because it made me sick. But something told me Ray would not take this news well.

"Is there a problem?" he snapped, wolfing down his own dinner.

It was as if he was goading me, itching for an argument. Lisa, head bowed, sliced her fishfingers into small sections. The only sound was the squeak of cutlery on their plates.

"I can't eat this," I whimpered. "I'm sorry."

Ray stifled a giggle.

"I think you can," he snorted. Then suddenly, his voice took on a menacing tone.

"And you will sit there until you do."

I dared to glance at Lisa for her reaction, but there was none. When their dinners were finished, they left the room. For the next three hours, I sat at the table, staring dolefully, incredulously, at my plate. The beans slowly solidified and the fishfingers went cold. The light faded outside. Yet still, I sat there. My shoulders ached and so did my heart. Running alongside my fear and alarm were feelings of mute shock. Nobody had ever spoken to me like that. I had never been treated like this before. At 8.45pm, Ray marched in and swept my plate up.

"You'd best get to bed," he snarled.

I didn't need telling twice. I scampered upstairs, with my heart clattering against my ribs, desperate for the safety of the bedroom. Hungry and frightened, I just wanted to go home.

****

When I heard Mum's car outside the following morning, my eyes swam with tears of relief. At last. Getting into the car, she asked, "Did you have a nice time?"

Not understanding why, I swallowed down my despair, and I nodded. I told her nothing of Karl's friend and his temper. I didn't mention I hadn't eaten and was starving. Maybe I thought she couldn't or wouldn't help. I was building a wall around me, with everyone I loved and who I thought had loved me, on the other side.

By the time we arrived home, I was revving up to a temper tantrum. Running into the kitchen, I was eaten up with a mix of hunger and anger. Looking wildly around me, I spotted my menu for the coming week, neatly printed out and pinned onto the fridge. It was a powerful symbol and the contrast between Lisa's house and my home could not have been starker. Here, I was somebody. There, I was a nobody. I was living between both of these worlds, and there was no overlap. The chasm could not have been wider, but I was expected, aged seven, to straddle it on my own. Furiously, I snatched the menu from under the fridge magnet and ripped it into small pieces. As it fluttered like snowflakes to the ground, Mum appeared behind me.

"What do you think you're doing?" she asked. "Bedroom. Now."

I stalked upstairs and got straight into my wardrobe. I could not see, as a child, that my behaviour was perfectly normal, given my circumstances. I could not argue back against Lisa and Karl and his friends so instead, I unleashed it at home where I felt safe.

Ripping up the menu was about taking control of a very small section of my life. But it was so out of character, so unexpected, that I felt no satisfaction, no sense of victory. I was disappointed with myself, and that was nearly as bad as disappointing my parents.

But it didn't stop there. When I was allowed to play out, I

ran off up the street, knowing full well I was crossing more boundaries and breaking more rules.

You must never go past the end of the street, Stace. It's too dangerous.

But what did I care? What did they care? They were happy to send me away to a place where I wasn't even wanted. They were unlikely to be too upset if I got lost or kidnapped or hit by a car.

"Stace, you must never do that again," Mum admonished, her face creased with worry.

But that was precisely the reaction I was hoping for. I *wanted* her to feel anxious and upset. I wanted her to feel the same as me. One weekend when I wasn't visiting Lisa, we went to our caravan in Scarborough. I was really looking forward to a little holiday and a chance to forget all about my problems. After unpacking, and arranging my beloved books in my bedroom, it was getting too late to play out. Instead, I set up a game of Scrabble for Dad and me. It was one of our favourite caravan games. We played for ages, whooping when we landed on the triple word scores, and then he said, "I think I'll have a break now, Stace. Watch a bit of telly."

And with that, my rage returned like the flick of a switch.

"I want to play another game!" I yelled, shocking even myself. "Why can't we ever do what I want?"

We nearly always did what I wanted. I knew, deep down, I was being unreasonable. Maybe I wanted to punish him. Maybe I wanted more control over my life. Either way, as I stamped around the caravan, Dad lost his temper, and shouted, "Calm down, Stace. Enough is enough!"

I rounded on him, eyes blazing. And suddenly, my voice was low and icy cold: "I don't know who you think you're shouting at," I said. "You are not even my Dad."

We both looked at each other for a moment, my own anguish and confusion mirrored in his eyes. I flounced off to bed, hating everyone, even myself. Especially myself. Back at school the following week, my anger continued to simmer. In class, when my teacher handed out worksheets, I stared stonily out of the window.

"Stace, why aren't you doing your sums?" she asked.

"Don't want to," I sulked. "And you can't make me."

I quite enjoyed the look of astonishment on her face. I had never in my life answered back at school. I'd always been a model pupil. But I found that I longed to get into trouble. I loved hearing her say how disappointed she was. After several warnings, I was finally sent out of class to stand in the corridor. What would once have been the ultimate shame, now became a glittering achievement. The deputy headteacher walked past me and raised her eyebrows in amazement when she recognised me.

"Is that Mrs Robinson's daughter, standing outside class in disgrace?" she asked, with exaggerated horror. "What did you do, Stace?"

I glared at her. For a start, I was not Mrs Robinson's daughter. She knew that. They all knew that, and always had. I had a different surname. It was obvious to them all, yet they had played along. I imagined them sniggering behind my back and I felt a stab of humiliation. The joke was on me.

"What happened?" she asked again.

It was a good question. What on earth had happened to me? I no longer knew who I was. I had lost my family, and by degrees, I was losing myself too.

5

IN ADDITION to the visits to Lisa's, the social worker organised for me to see my birth father. For reasons I didn't understand, these visits were to take place at a contact centre, in Oldham, and would be supervised by social services.

"At no time will you be left alone with him," she said.

If her comment was supposed to reassure me, it did not. I had no idea why or how he presented a risk to me.

Walking into the room, at a contact centre in Oldham town centre, I was met by an abundance of toys stacked on shelves and teetering in piles on the carpet. To my delight, I spotted a sponge football, and immediately began practising keepy-ups. I knew the man was sitting on a chair, but I didn't even look at him. I didn't want to see his bristly nose hairs and his cold dark eyes. More than that, I didn't want the reminder that I had the same eyes too. The social worker made several fruitless attempts to bridge the silence.

"How about we all build a Lego house?" she suggested. "You, me and your father, Nigel?"

But I was determined to focus only on my football. And

my father seemed inexplicably furious, muttering a stream of complaints at the social worker. For a moment, I panicked that perhaps I had somehow caught my temper tantrums from him, just as I'd once caught chickenpox from a boy at school. It made perfect sense. I'd been a calm, happy little girl until that day in the park. He was clearly an angry man. Perhaps his fury was infectious. Or, worse, maybe it was genetic. Like the chin, and the eyes, I'd inherited his rage too. A shudder ran through me, and I dropped my ball.

"Please can I go home?" I asked the social worker in a small voice. "I don't feel well."

A second visit was arranged, at the same contact centre, but it was a carbon copy of the first. My father was annoyed, and I spent my time playing with the football and the toys, avoiding his eyes. By not speaking to him at all, I hoped he might decide these meetings were not worth his time. And it seemed I'd got my own way, because afterwards the social worker told me I didn't need to go back. And yet, that was, perversely, a kick in the teeth. As much as I didn't want to see the man, I wanted him to want to see me. He was supposed to be my father after all. Nobody liked me, not my foster family and not my birth family. I was, I told myself, unlovable.

My eighth birthday came and, as usual, I was indulged with a small mountain of gifts.

"Happy Birthday!" sang my parents.

I tried on my new football kit and I laced up my new boots. They were nice. It was all nice. But what I wanted, was to be loved. What I needed, was a place where I belonged. No amount of gifts could compensate for the feelings of uncertainty and sadness that clouded everything I did. And with these thoughts jamming my brain daily, my schoolwork and behaviour suffered. Comments which had once filled me with pride now sliced right through my soul:

"Here's Mrs Robinson and her daughter.'

"Let Mrs Robinson's daughter take that letter."

"I hope that's not Mrs Robinson's daughter on detention.'

I wanted to stand on the teacher's desk and scream, "I am not Mrs Robinson's daughter. It's all been a lie!"

Yet conversely, I wished it could be kept secret too. I didn't want anyone to know the truth. I felt like an imposter, barging into my own life, where I had no business being. I had built my entire identity around being 'Mrs Robinson's daughter' and now, like a precious glass vase, it was shattered. And it could not be pieced back together. Who was I? Where had I come from? Where did I belong? At home, too, my behaviour continued to spiral. One afternoon, after a visit to Lisa's, I went straight to my wardrobe. I seemed to spend half my life in there these days. I refused to go downstairs for my tea, and instead, while they were all eating, I crept out onto the landing. Downstairs, I could hear the chatter around the dining table, the soft clink of crockery, my father's laugh, a little louder than the rest. Inside, I ached and ached. I longed to be a part of it. I desperately wished I could rewind. Yet in my heart, I knew it could not happen.

Well, Lou-Lou. I'm your dad.

In the doorway of my parents' bedroom, I spotted their money jar, a large whisky bottle, usually filled with coppers and small change. But today, I noticed a £10 note, folded into the neck of the bottle. A hot, itchy resentment spread like insects crawling across my skin. I had never stolen anything in my life, and yet calmly, I poked my finger into the bottle and just managed to grab the note. Good job I had such small hands I thought grimly, as though this was a sort of justifiable revenge mission. I ran downstairs and out of the house before anyone had a chance to notice. I didn't stop running until I reached the shop.

"What would you like?" the assistant asked.

I had a flashback to my father, offering me sweets and then bringing me here for strawberry bon bons. Again, I realised he was the only one to keep his promises. Today, with a £10 note in my hand, I was bowled over by the sheer cornucopia of choice. Sometime later, my arms overflowing, I reflected on a valuable lesson: £10 bought me a lot of sweets. But it bought me no joy. I marched down the street, teeth gritted, every step garnished with rage. I knocked on the door of my pal Laura's house, and could not wait to show off my illegal stash. But again, there was no delight, only a hazy sense of vengeance.

"Wow!" she said, at first impressed.

But as the treats kept on coming, her face grew serious.

"Stace, how did you buy all this?" she asked. "Tell me the honest truth."

Unsmiling, I rolled my eyes and opened a packet of Haribo. I was just starting to feel a bit sick when I heard the front doorbell ring, followed by the sound of my mother's voice. Laura looked shame faced.

"I only told them because I don't want you getting into trouble," she said.

But to me, she had landed me right in it. I should have known, I told myself furiously. I couldn't trust anyone anymore, Laura included.

"You're grounded again," my foster mother told me. "When will you ever learn?"

In my bedroom, I grabbed my football and climbed into my wardrobe. The anger trickled away through my fingers like water, leaving behind an unbearable sadness. I hugged my beloved football to me like a shield. It was all I had left.

* * * *

My ninth birthday passed in April 1998, and the visits with Lisa continued. And though I grew to quite like her, I did not like her boyfriend or his friends.

Most times I visited, there was a cluster of adults sitting either in the living room watching films, or at the dining table, smoking and laughing about grown-up stuff. To a small girl, they were intimidating and scary.

"Oi, you should tell your foster parents you want to come and live with Lisa," Ray said, nodding in my direction. "Why do you want to live with them stuck-up idiots anyway?"

I swallowed hard. I did not dare answer him back, yet I squirmed with guilt for not speaking up for my family. Why had I let him talk about them like that? He had never even met them.

"Oi kid," he said, from his spot on the sofa. "I'm talking to you."

Gulping back tears, I looked to Lisa for support. But she

had simply merged into the background. She might just as well have been a cushion or a lamp. She rarely spoke. She rarely even looked up. Yet she was all I had and, during my visits, I stuck to her like a little limpet, terrified of finding myself alone with Karl's friends. Even when she went to the toilet, I followed her upstairs and perched anxiously on the top step, outside the bathroom door.

"Haha, look at this weird kid," laughed Deano, spotting me huddled on the landing.

From then on, I was known as the weird kid. They spoke about me like I was some kind of disease, as though if they came too close, they might catch whatever bad luck I was carrying around with me.

"About time you started calling her Mum, not Lisa," Karl told me. "She's your Mum. Not that Claire Robinson."

Lisa nodded along, like an obedient puppy. Confusion swirled like fog around me. How many mothers did I have? But I dared not disobey him.

"Ok," I said quietly. "Ok, Mum."

The word, once so familiar and comforting, felt like a stone in my mouth, awkward and sharp. I pictured Mum's face, imagined her crumpling with tears as she heard me call someone else her name. I could only hope she'd never find out. It felt like a betrayal, a total sell-out. At my next visit, Ray served up rubbery burgers, and I baulked.

"Eat it!" Ray snapped.

Again, I looked to Lisa, and again, she ignored me. She seemed to melt into her chair and diminish, as though she was trying to disappear into the fabric. I was struck, as she shrank back, how slim and slight she was, just like me. But I did not want a resemblance. I did not want a connection. I just wanted to go home.

My problem was not with Lisa but rather with her unwillingness or inability to stand up to her partner and friends. As an adult, I have some empathy with her. I appreciate she could not fight her own corner, so how on earth could she fight mine? She put her boyfriend and his friends first, before me, because she did not know any other way. Time and time again, she failed me, but I don't believe it was done with malice. She just didn't know how to be a parent. But as a nine-year-old, the reasons why did not matter, and I saw only that she was not on my side. Her lack of stature was both physical and psychological, the slightness of her physique mirrored in her failure to protect me. That afternoon, I sat at the table until my burger was cold and congealed. Mercifully, bedtime came, and Ray decided on balance he would rather get rid of me than see me flounder any longer.

"Bed," he ordered, and I scampered off upstairs.

Because I dared not express my frustrations to Lisa or Karl or his friends, I saved them all up, a whole list of grievances, until I got home. By the time Mum collected me, I was boiling over with rage.

"What's the matter?" she asked. "Did you not have a nice time?"

My face was hot with exasperation.

"What would you care?" I snapped. "What would anybody care?"

The social worker visited a few days later. With bad timing

on my part, I opened the front door to her, and so was stuck facing her in the hallway.

"Shall we sit down?" Mum suggested, shepherding me into the living room. "The social worker would like to know how you're getting on."

But already, I had tuned out. I didn't want to hear any of this. Instead of sitting, I walked to the far wall and turned to face it.

"How did the last visit go?" she asked.

Silence.

"Did you have fun?"

Silence.

"Do you enjoy sleeping over?"

Silence.

"Stace," she said eventually. "I am trying to help you. Please talk to me. I just want to find out how it's going at your Mum's house?"

With this, I spun to face her, my eyes flashing. When the words finally came, it was like spitting venom.

"Her name is Lisa. She is *not* my mother."

With that, I ran from the room, upstairs and straight into my wardrobe. I refused to come out for the rest of the evening and the next day, at school, I was sent out of class for being cheeky. When Mum spotted me in the corridor, she groaned.

"Stace, you can't keep behaving like this," she said. "You're grounded for another week. No playing out. No football. No Irish dancing. We've got to get tough on this behaviour. It just won't do."

Grounded again. Well, I had an answer for that. The

moment we arrived home, I ran upstairs and packed my Spice Girls pencilcase and my football stickers book into a carrier bag. I tried to fit my football in, but it was too big. I changed my school shoes for my footie boots too. If I could only take one set of footwear, it had to be my boots.

"I am running away," I announced loudly, as I clomped furiously down the stairs.

I slammed the front door loudly and ran all the way to the top of the street. At the junction, there were several large trees, and my plan was to hide behind the biggest, to make my family think I had disappeared completely. I was too scared to go any further. But maybe, just maybe, if they thought I'd gone for good, they'd realise how much they loved me and they might stop sending me away to Lisa's. I had to stand very still behind the tree, to avoid my arms and legs poking out and giving the game away.

I didn't even feel confident of getting my sticker book out to brush up on my player statistics. What if my elbow jutted out and I was exposed? But after a while, it got boring hiding on my own, and it grew chilly, too. Where was the search party? The police sirens? The helicopter? And then, there was a rustle, and Donna's face peeped around the side of the tree.

"How long are you going to stand there, Stace?" she asked. "We're all wondering what you're doing out here. Come on home. I'll make you scrambled eggs."

I was so relieved to see her that I forgot about my grand plan. I didn't care that they'd seen through it all along. With my hand in hers, I skipped down the street, just grateful someone cared enough to come and bring me home. That was all I craved.

* * * *

At the social worker's next visit, I clammed up again. She peppered me with questions and suggestions, but I refused even to look at her. With my back turned, and my eyes closed, I made a mental list of the football results for the previous weekend. By focussing on the scores, and not on the conversation, I could almost pretend all this wasn't happening. Football was my escape, my saviour.

Everton 1, West Ham, 0. Leeds 2, Middlesbrough, 0. What was the Newcastle score? There were goals. But how many?

"Stace?" she was saying. "Can I please ask you about these visits. I need to know what you would like to do and where you would like to live."

Spurs 3, Coventry, 2.

My parents were mortified at my lack of manners. After the social worker had left, they handed me a blank sheet of paper and a pen.

"The social worker has asked you to write down who you would like to live with," Mum said.

Her eyes glistened with tears, but in that moment, I felt only my own pain. I wanted so much to wound her. To give her a small taste, just a droplet, of the anguish I felt. But could I really go that far? Could I say I wanted to live with Lisa, as revenge? Then I had a sharp reminder of Karl, cornering me on the landing:

You know, you should really be living here. She's your mum. You belong with her, not with them.

I was too afraid to cross him. Too frightened of the reper-cussions. And the pressure of having to choose where I wanted to live, having to pick out a favourite family, weighed so heavy on my young shoulders. It was too much. Taking the pen, I scrawled: 'I would like to live with Lisa.'

And then I burst into tears. I didn't want to live with Lisa. Surely from my behaviour it was obvious that I didn't. What I wanted was for my parents to step in and sort all of this out. I was so confused I felt physically sick much of the time.

In the weeks afterwards, the tension in the house built and built. It was like a heatwave, the mercury shooting up the barometer, the temperatures sliding off the scale. There was a storm brewing and there was trouble ahead. I didn't know what form it might take but, like dirty grey clouds rumbling in the distance, I knew it was coming.

One night, as I lay in bed, I heard my parents arguing downstairs. That in itself was shocking. They never, ever, fell out. It was unusual even to hear raised voices, and this was a full-blown row.

"We should say that. We should just be honest. See what the judge thinks."

"No! No! It will cause even more trouble."

"But what about Stace? What are we going to do?"

More shocking still was the revelation that I was at the centre of the problem. Later on, I heard muffled sobs as my mother cried into her pillow. The warning bells clanged loudly in my head. Warning me of what, I did not know.

In September 1999, I began year six, my final year of primary school. Along with my pals, I began preparing for the transition to high school. Despite myself, and despite everything that was going on at home, I was filled with excitement. We went along to the high school for an induction day, and I made more new friends. As we walked into the hall, the most popular girl in the entire year patted the chair next to her and said, "Stace, I've saved you a seat next to me."

Smiling broadly, I slipped onto the chair and suddenly, I had a feeling everything was going to be okay. The problems at home could all be swept away like old leaves, I told myself. Mum and Dad would start smiling again. The social workers would disappear. Life would soon be back on track.

6

EVEN AS I arrived home, perhaps I could feel it. The walls whispering in warning. The door creaking in protest. My football, in the hallway, staring dolefully back at me.

You're not going to like this, Stace.

"Stace, the social worker is coming today," Mum said stiffly, as I hung my coat up. "I'll do you a quick snack before she gets here, okay?"

Inwardly, I recoiled. There was something about Mum's tone, standoffish, formal. As if she was already distancing herself.

"Today, it's really important that you sit down and listen to what she has to say," Mum added. "Please, love."

She sounded so defeated, so weary, that I simply nodded in reply. Her lethargy was infectious, and I could not find it in me to be annoyed. When I heard the doorbell, I went to sit on the sofa, and hoped that whatever was happening would at least happen quickly. I was hoping to meet my pals for a game of football before tea. The social worker took her place on a chair opposite and opened her file with a rustle.

"Well, Stace," she said, with a smile. "Big news today."

Her smile did not reach her eyes. It did not even reach the ends of her mouth. And I felt suddenly sick with dread.

"As you will know, your foster parents and your mother both made applications to the court for you to live with them. And the courts have made a decision…"

Liverpool 2, Manchester United 0. Coventry 2, Derby 0. Sunderland 0, Leeds 2.

But no matter how much I focussed on the football results, I could not drown her out. Like a whining drill she forced her way into my brain.

"You will live with your birth mother, Lisa, for two weeks at first, and we will see how you get on."

Without a word, I climbed down from my seat and crawled under the coffee table.

West Ham 0, Everton 2. Chelsea – Oh, who did Chelsea play?

"So," she said brightly. "I imagine you're going to be very busy packing! Very busy indeed! What an exciting time for you!"

I was still under the table, teeth clattering, hands trembling, when she left.

* * * *

Waiting until it was quiet in the hallway, I crept out from under the table and ran upstairs, into my room and into my wardrobe. So, they were getting rid of me completely. Scrubbed out like a dirty stain. Incinerated like toxic waste. The visits to Lisa's had been like slow self-mutilation, cutting my fingers off one by one. Then amputating an arm. A leg maybe. Now, it was the whole thing. I was being erased. Cradling my football in my arms, I sobbed and sobbed.

"This will serve them right," I told myself eventually. "They'll miss me when I'm gone."

I did not appreciate that the Robinsons had wanted me to stay; that their own application had been rejected by the court. I blamed them, as my parents, for not trying hard enough. My own pain was overwhelming, and I had no capacity for theirs also. A desperate plan was forming in my head. I would stay with Lisa for two weeks and then I would come home. How would I get home? It was a long way. I'd have to think about that. But this was my big chance to reject my parents, as they had rejected me. Teach them a lesson. Reminding myself that it was only temporary, I rinsed my face in the bathroom and went downstairs. Mum was sitting at the kitchen table and from her red, puffy eyes, I could see she'd been crying too.

"I'll be okay," I said, with false brightness. "I might enjoy myself."

She did not reply. Soon after, I came home to find Dad carrying empty carboard boxes in from the garage.

"We need to start packing your stuff, Stace," he said heavily. "You're going on Saturday."

In that moment, my resolve cracked and dissolved. I did not want to go. Not for two weeks. Not for two days. Not for two minutes. My insides lurched as I watched Dad carefully lifting my books and toys into boxes. Why so many things for a two-week stay? Why did I need my toys? What was going on? I didn't ask because I didn't want the answer. When he picked up my beloved David Beckham book, something snapped inside me. It was like a rubber band, pulled too tight, pinging back against my heart. Unable to watch any more, I climbed inside my wardrobe, scrunched myself up as small as I could, and pulled the door shut.

Only now, with just a few days to spare, I saw the foolishness of my plan. I didn't want to go away. I didn't want to hurt my parents. I just wanted things to stay as they were. Hugging my football close, I formulated a second plan. From that very moment, my behaviour would be impeccable. I would be so good and so polite that they would be persuaded into keeping me after all. Climbing back out of the wardrobe, I said to Dad, "Do we need any more boxes out of the garage? I'll fetch them."

"No, love," he said sadly. "We're doing okay, I think."

After we'd eaten, that evening, I helped clear the table. And while my mother loaded the dishwasher, I got the dustpan and brush out and swept the crumbs from under the dining chairs.

"Thanks Stace," she smiled. "You're a good girl."

Usually, before I went to bed, Mum laid out my clothes ready for the next day. But I was determined to beat her to it. I ran upstairs, pulling underwear and socks out of my drawers, along with my school uniform; a green skirt, green cardigan and white shirt. I got myself undressed and climbed into bed, five minutes before my 8pm deadline, without a word of complaint.

The next day, and the next, I was a model child. But all week, boxes of my stuff squatted in the hallway like unwelcome houseguests, overstaying their invite. On Friday evening, after my bath, I watched from my window as Dad loaded each box into the back of our family Mercedes estate. My life. Reduced to boxes. Reduced to this. I blinked back tears, and yet still, I was convinced I could salvage this.

I barely slept that night and the next morning, as reassuring shafts of light crept into my bedroom, I was wide awake, adrenaline rushing through me like a fast river. Tiptoeing out, so as not to wake Donna, I crept downstairs and made my own breakfast, Weetos and a glass of chocolate milk. Afterwards, I washed my own dishes. They couldn't send me away now – could they? There was a noise in the hallway and I half expected to hear Dad unloading the car. Instead, he called, "Can you check the drying rack for the rest of Stace's clothes, Claire? We need to leave really within the next hour."

In that moment, I felt as though I was made of porcelain and there were tiny hairline cracks criss-crossing around my body. Any moment now, a huge crack would split me right down the middle and I would break apart completely. Determined to keep battling, right to the end, I wiped the splashes of milk from the dining table. As I rinsed out the dishcloth, Mum came into the kitchen.

"Oh Stace," she whispered.

Falling to her knees, she wrapped her arms around me, and the tears flowed from us both.

"It's time," Dad said, from the doorway. "Come on, love."

I had to run back upstairs for my jacket and, as I took one last look at my room, it seemed to pull at me on all sides, desperate for me to stay. The walls themselves seem to quietly weep.

Don't go, Stace. Please don't go.

But outside, Dad was already in the car, reversing out of the driveway. As we drove away from the house, I looked out at the park, and at the pyramid of sand, now partially collapsed after the builders had dug into it. There could not have been a more painful metaphor. All through the journey, I did not say a word. I could not even recall the mid-week football scores. It felt like the end of all happiness.

7

ARRIVING AT Lisa's, Dad jumped out of the car and kept himself busy unloading boxes and carrying bags. I stood on the pavement, lost and out of place in every way. Lisa's dog growled menacingly from the hallway, a portent of what was to come.

"Come in," Lisa smiled. "I'll put the dog in the kitchen and show you your bedroom."

I looked to Dad for his approval, but as he put the final box down in the doorway, he said, "I'll be on my way now."

He turned and strode away quickly, without even giving me a hug. As I folded with pain, it felt like the final twist of the knife. I realise, looking back, he was probably trying to hide his own tears. But I would far rather have witnessed his distress, testament of his love for me, than see him slink away, as though he couldn't get rid of me fast enough.

"Come and see your room," Lisa said again, and so with my heart and feet dragging, I followed her upstairs. She and I were the only ones in the house; Karl had gone out somewhere. She opened my bedroom door with a small flourish of her hand and I tried to force a smile. She had made such an effort. The walls were painted alternately lime and lemon with new matching curtains. There was a set of drawers with a small portable TV on top. But no wardrobe. No sanctuary. No safe place.

"It's lovely," I mumbled. "Thanks."

And it was lovely. It really was. The only problem was it wasn't mine. I had a bedroom, back home. I had a Mum and Dad. I had a family. And already, I missed them so much.

"I'll leave you to unpack," Lisa said uncertainly.

And then she was gone. Though I didn't want to unpack alone, I didn't feel comfortable with her either. She and I were virtual strangers. We'd never really had a full conversation and now here I was, living with her. My whole body began to tingle with anxiety as reality smacked me in the face. *I am living here, with Lisa.* My future stretched before me like a tightrope strung across a canyon. So precarious, I was doomed to fall.

Aston Villa 3, Coventry 2. Liverpool 3, Newcastle 0. Michael Owen scored…

But try as I might, I couldn't lose myself in football stats forever. I had to face this and if I didn't unpack, nobody would do it for me.

My new room was small and, looking around, I had no idea where I would store all my belongings. One by one, I took my books out of the boxes and tried to stack them up on top of the drawers. But they just didn't look right. They didn't fit in here. My David Beckham book fell off the end and onto the carpet, and Beckham's face gazed mournfully at me from the back cover.

When are we going home? When can I get back on the shelf above the bed?

"We're only here for two weeks," I reminded him. "Then we can go back."

But I wasn't sure I even believed that myself. My rosettes and certificates were stacked neatly at the side of the box, but again, I could find no space for them in this room. And who would be interested in my achievements anyway?

Reaching back into a box, I saw that the clay house I'd made at school, one of my favourite belongings, had been smashed in the move. The roof was caved in, and the door was broken, and in many ways, I felt the same myself. Pushing the remaining boxes under the bed, I lay on the duvet and sobbed. Even the bed didn't smell right; Mum used a different fabric softener, and though I'd never really taken much notice before, I longed for that scent now.

At home, everything always smelled so clean. Here, there was an over-emphasis on fragrance; the hallway smelled of air-freshener and there was a strong odour of cleaning products in my bedroom. Maybe it was just very clean. But it felt to me as though it was masking something. Bereft and betrayed, I continued to cry.

It somehow felt that this whole process had been a set-up, right from that first visit. This had been the plan all along, and I had fallen for it. Furious at my own stupidity, angry at the deception, I remained curled up on the bed until I heard voices downstairs. Karl shouted, "Don't even think about putting any posters up. Those walls are freshly painted."

I thought of Robbie Fowler and Eric Cantona, pinned to

my wall back home, and a fresh wave of longing engulfed me. Soon after, another voice yelled, "Come on, weird kid, food's ready."

My heart sank. I wondered whether Mum had sent my weekly menu, and if Lisa would follow it. I doubted it somehow.

"Coming," I called, anxious not to get into trouble.

"Sausage and mash," Karl announced.

The greasy sausage smell was an assault on my senses. I did my best not to retch at the table, but I knew there was no way I could manage a single mouthful.

"Well, you'll sit there until you eat it," said Karl. "And that's final."

I tried cutting the sausages into very tiny slices and hiding them under the potato. But Karl spotted what I was doing, grabbed my knife and flicked the sausage back out again. He banged the knife down onto the table so that my plate jumped and hissed, "Just eat it."

That first night, I sat on my own at the table until the light faded. The gristle in the sausage glistened in the dark and a shiver of disgust ran through me. The adults drifted away, and the room grew dark and gloomy. I didn't even get up to switch on the light. I saw no point. I didn't want to look around me. When I was eventually allowed to go to bed, my head was drooping with exhaustion and my stomach was growling with hunger.

"Night Stace," Lisa said, as we passed on the landing.

"Night… Mum," I replied.

The word felt just as uncomfortable and unwieldy as always. Yet I knew, from now on, I had to use it. My own mother was gone and this woman, who barely made eye contact with me, had taken her place.

In my bedroom, I messed about with the wire coathanger which was stuck in the back of the TV, until I got a signal. There were no subscription channels here. No football repeats. No European matches. Instead, I half-watched a show about late night policing, which did nothing to calm my jangling nerves. When nobody came to say goodnight, I was simultaneously relieved and disappointed. Nobody seemed to care that my TV was still blaring at nearly midnight. This household was a curious mix of tyranny and liberty. On the one hand, I was practically force-fed, I was teased, taunted, and bullied. Yet in many respects, I could do as I pleased. There were no bedtimes, no rules, no structure. There was a complete lack of routine. And alongside it, there was a complete lack of love. Even aged 10 I realised the reason nobody came to switch out my light was that nobody really cared. The indifference was worse even than the hostility. They had probably forgotten I was there.

In the early hours, I climbed out of bed and wedged my door shut with the end of the drawers. I didn't feel safe here. I certainly didn't feel welcome.

* * * *

The following morning, I woke with my usual Sunday morning enthusiasm before realising, with a thud, that I was not in my own bed. There would be no trip to the car boot sale. No Sunday afternoon football. No cheesy pizza.

David Beckham seemed to glare accusingly from the top of the drawers:

Why are we still here?

"Not my fault," I mumbled. "I don't like it either."

Sitting up in bed, I pulled my duvet around me and sighed. In my mind's eye, I could imagine the scene back home, as clearly as if it was being screened on the telly in front of me. There was Donna, in her pyjamas, making scrambled eggs for two.

Come on Stace! I've done double portions. You can butter the toast.

Mum was at the sink, snapping on her rubber gloves, ready to scrub the kitchen worktops.

I've saved the white bread for you, Stace, last two slices!

Dad was in the hallway, pulling on his coat, preparing for a stroll down to the local shop.

Where's my special girl? Who wants strawberry bon bons?

My heart yearned to be with them again. I was slowly beginning to accept we were not related by blood. We shared no resemblance, no genetic link. But they were my family all the same. They had raised me and loved me, and I loved them back. The connection was visceral and the pull to go home was umbilical, regardless of whether we were biologically linked. It was so strong; it was almost magnetic.

When my hunger got the better of me, I climbed out of bed, noticing my new mother had not picked out an outfit for me to wear. I pulled on my favourite joggers and a football shirt and went downstairs. There was nobody in the kitchen and neither could I find any Weetos in the cupboards. I settled for a slice of toast in the end, thankful that Donna had showed me how to use a toaster in our cooking lessons. Though my hunger eased, my anxiety did not. I felt as though I was sneaking around in someone else's kitchen, masquerading as Lisa's daughter. After I'd washed my plate, I scurried back upstairs and closed my bedroom door. I spent the rest of the morning sitting on my bed, waiting for something to happen. At home, there was always a plan, and I was constantly entertained. Here, there was nothing, and the loneliness lingered like the damp I could smell in my bedroom walls. Early in the afternoon, Mum tapped on my door.

"Stace, I'm doing spaghetti hoops if you'd like some?" she asked.

"No thank you," I mumbled. "I'll just have toast."

Downstairs, she and I sat at the table without speaking. She seemed as much at a loss with me, as I was with her. I had moved in, and I was a member of the household. But we were living alongside each other and not together.

"Do you fancy going to the shop?" she asked eventually. "Get some sweets?"

I shook my head miserably.

"No thanks," I muttered.

I stared at her face and wondered whether I would slowly turn into her. She was, after all, my closest biological relative. I knew nothing of the nature-nurture debate as an 11-year-old, but already I could feel my happy, confident self, retreating, and a timid, nervous girl taking my place. It was as though someone had taken all the effervescence from my old life and popped every bubble. And now here I was, flattened and frightened. Physically and mentally I was shrinking into a smaller version of myself. In the afternoon, Mum's boyfriend and friends arrived.

"Wanna play footie?" Karl asked me.

My mouth opened and closed as I wrestled internally with the offer. I desperately wanted to play football. And yet, I felt somehow disloyal, as if I was betraying my family by agreeing.

"Come on," Karl said impatiently. "I haven't got all day."

Guided more by fear than enthusiasm, I followed him out to the back garden with my ball under my arm. But the moment my foot connected with the ball, a calm came over me and my worries floated away, into the air and over the garden hedge. Playing football gave me a natural high, certainly. I loved the elation and the thrill. I enjoyed the admiration too; not many girls played football back then, very few as dedicated as me, and I got lots of compliments for showing off my skills. But it was more than that. Having a football at my feet was almost a sense of relief; it gave me balance and peace. It was the nearest feeling I got to being at home.

* * * *

The next day, Monday, I was back at school. Despite the distance, the social workers had decided I should remain at the same primary school, because my time there was almost over. I had been pleased by the news at first; I was keen to see my friends. More than anything, I wanted to see my mother, working in the school office. I had half-thought out a plan where I might persuade her to let me go home.

"You ready?" Karl asked. "It's a long way. We're going to miss the bus."

I had really hoped Mum might take me. I was wary of Karl. But she was busy so I nodded and followed him out of the door. The bus journey seemed to last forever, and it was tense, too. Karl did not speak except to bark a few orders.

"Sit up straight. Don't mumble. Pick your bag up."

I got the impression he didn't like me very much, and I wasn't sure what I could do about that. I couldn't wait to arrive at school, to run right into the office and throw myself into my mother's arms. But, as I walked through the gates, I was flooded with doubt. Even before I reached the office, I knew I had got this all wrong.

"Mum?" I said, in a small voice, as I reached the door.

She looked up and smiled, but it was a polite smile, and slightly strained. The sort of smile she might use for another pupil she didn't know too well. One who had, with the best intentions, overstepped the mark in some respect.

"How are you?" she asked, ushering me along the corridor. "Is everything going well?"

Maybe it was my own perception, but I felt the question was framed in such a way that I could not tell the truth.

"Yeah," I mumbled.

It was torture, sitting in class all day, knowing Mum was in the office just metres away. I was bursting with things to tell her.

I've no wardrobe, nowhere to hide! There's no menu. No Weetos. No cheesy pizzas. My clay house broke. My David Beckham book doesn't fit in there…

The list was endless. Mum could fix all these problems, I knew it. She could fix anything. And what I needed to tell her, most of all:

I miss you. I miss you all. Please let me come home.

The end of the school day was the worst moment of the lot. I had to watch Mum going home without me, back to the life I'd once had. I was torn in two, knowing I was not allowed to go with her. It was agony to have experienced such happiness, and then to have it snatched away. I remembered the 'Bullseye' reruns that Dad liked to watch on telly:

Let's have a look at what you could have won!

The next day, and the one after, I felt worse than ever. I hated being in such close proximity to reminders from the past. It was as though someone was waving a wonderful prize under my nose then plucking it away at the last minute. My new mum sent me with a packed lunch, but it was a poor imitation of my usual selection of treats. One day, there was a ham sandwich and cheese and onion crisps, which I could not eat. The next, it was corned beef and a bruised banana. I was so appalled, I had to close my eyes as I scraped it into the bin.

"What's the matter, Stace?" Mum asked, as she walked past me in the dining hall.

"I don't like my packed lunch," I muttered. "It's just not the same as before."

The teachers, too, treated me differently. I was not chosen to run errands or to take messages between classes. I was no longer 'Mrs Robinson's daughter.' My identity had been stolen and smashed to bits. My family had gone. My home had gone. I no longer knew who I was. The only constant was my football.

A couple of days later, Karl grew tired both of the long bus journey and of my company. Instead, social services booked a taxi to take me to school. When I found out I had to go on my own in the taxi, I was horror-struck.

"Please, can someone come with me?" I asked Mum.

She shrugged.

"You'll be okay, the taxi driver will look after you."

But I became obsessed that the taxi driver might kidnap me. When he beeped outside the house, that first morning, I became rigid with fear. The driver had a huge moustache which inexplicably confirmed my suspicions that he was not to be trusted. I spent the whole journey with my eye on the door, ready to jump out if needed.

"Have a good day," he smiled, as he dropped me outside the school gates, and I was equally as perplexed as I was relieved.

One morning, a new driver came and to my alarm, he took me to a completely different school. I had no idea where I was. At first, I thought it was all part of the kidnap plan. Then, he explained he had mixed me up with another pupil.

"Don't worry, I'll take you to the right school now," he said. "You'll be a bit late, that's all."

I didn't care about being late. I hated being at school so close to my foster mother. Yet I dreaded being at home, where I wasn't wanted. Even with the threat of kidnap hanging in the air, being in the taxi was probably the best place for me.

8

FOR MY 11th birthday, Mum presented me with a dolls' house. I thanked her politely, but deep down I was baffled and upset. I hadn't played with dolls for years and this was a gift more suited to a child half my age. I saw it as a clear reflection of just how little she knew me or considered me.

Aside from the present, there was no celebration, no cake, no party, no birthday tea. That night in my bedroom, I idly picked up one of the small dolls from the house and put her in a different room. With one single wrist action, I could scoop her up and plonk her in a completely different environment.

It mirrored exactly what had happened to me. A giant hand had swooped into my home and transported me here to an alien place. The question was, how to get back again? Gently, I lifted the dolly and popped her back in her original room. If only it were that easy for me.

If school was harrowing for me, my home life was even more so. The only bonus – and it was a small one – was that Mum got rid of the dog after it apparently attacked someone. But I was fast learning that the adults here were even more formidable than the dog.

I felt as though I was in the way all the time, too. In direct contrast to the order and calm at my old house, this new place was chaotic and noisy. Karl and his friends were always around, and I spent all my time either playing football outside or shut away in my bedroom, with only my books for company.

At home, I'd had a strict routine which included a bath every night after tea. Mum or Dad would wash and rinse my hair once a week, brushing and blow-drying before bed. Though I was 11, I had never washed my own hair without supervision. I was the baby of the family in every sense, with my parents fussing over me like I was a China doll. At my new house, I had to grow up instantly.

Nobody told me to get a bath, or to wash my hair. Nobody noticed if I forgot to clean my teeth. Some days, I was grubby, my fingernails were dirty, and my long hair was lank and dull. I needed a shower. But in such a disorganised house, with so many strangers coming and going, I was reluctant to spend time in the bathroom. What if somebody walked in on me? What if someone else needed the bathroom and I got into trouble? I was frightened even of poking my head out of my bedroom door in case it was the wrong thing to do.

In this house, every small movement was exaggerated and amplified. Even coughing, I panicked in case I got into trouble. And during those hours, sitting at the dining table, watching my food grow cold, I felt so out of place and unwelcome. I might as well have been an ugly piece of furniture or an unwanted pet.

I used up too much oxygen. I took up too much room. And yet at the same time, I was becoming less and less. I felt as small and insignificant as a tiny bug. Nobody noticed me. Nobody cared. I was beginning to understand why my mother seemed to shrink back into her chair. Because now, the same thing was happening to me. Perhaps it was a cry for help; a plea for someone to reach out to me. Or maybe I had already given up on myself, for slowly, I stopped showering altogether. I gave up washing my hair. I did not clean my teeth. I had no interest in my appearance at all. I hid myself away in my bedroom, surfacing only when I was under orders.

One evening, Deano yelled my name up the stairs, and I went down to find he'd cooked sausage and oven chips. After last time, Mum knew I didn't like sausages. But I knew not to expect any support from her. So I was resigned to sitting it out quietly, until bedtime. But then, Deano said, "I've cooked your meal. You should eat it. You're an ungrateful little cow."

Tears pricked at my eyeballs, but I held them back. I had the feeling crying would only irritate him more.

"Are you gonna eat it or not?" he demanded.

With my stomach roiling, I shook my head. And it was no good, the tears spilled over, down my cheeks and onto my plate.

"Stand up," he bawled suddenly, sliding his belt from his jeans. I had never in my life been smacked or punished physically in any way and the shock hit me more forcefully than the belt itself. As the leather thwacked onto the back of my legs, I felt a searing pain both outside and in.

"Get to bed!" he thundered.

With the door wedged shut, I lay on my bed and wept.

I could not stay here. I just couldn't.

Every time I heard a creak on the stairs, I panicked Deano was coming to hit me again. For hours, I was too uneasy to fall asleep. Even my comfort habit of reciting football scores had deserted me, because the season had just finished. Without sports subscriptions, I couldn't watch replays or European channels. Instead, I tried to focus on statistics.

Manchester United won the league.

Kevin Phillips got the Golden Boot.

Relegated teams were Wimbledon, Watford and… oh, who else was relegated? I can't remember…

When I finally dozed off, I dreamed I was climbing the sand mountain in the park. But with each step, I was sinking further and further in the sand and soon it was up to my knees, and then my waist. The more I tried to pull myself out, the lower I sank.

"Help!" I yelled. "Someone help me get out!"

As the sand reached my chin, my heart pounded in panic, and I heard a voice from the grass below.

"Hi Lou-Lou, I'm your dad."

"Help!" I screamed again. "If you're really my dad, you would help me."

But he just stared impassively with those cold eyes, and I was sucked in, even lower. I could taste sand, gritty and coarse between my teeth and, in horror, I knew I was going to die here. Then, with seconds to spare, I heard Mum Lisa's voice.

"Hiya Stace."

She was perched on a dining chair on top of the pyramid, with Karl at her side. For a moment, Mum watched as I choked. Then she just shrugged and as she turned back to Karl, the sand covered the ponytail on top of my head.

****

When I woke the next morning, I was determined to do everything I could to get back home. Back to my real parents who, ironically, were not my parents at all. A little of my old spark flickered again as I came up with what I thought was an ingenious plan. If I was naughty – really, horribly, outrageously, naughty – surely Mum would send me back. Karl, Ray and Deano would quickly get sick of my behaviour. And they would be only too pleased to throw me out. Anxious to put my strategy straight into practice, I dashed out onto the landing and yelled over the bannister at the top of my voice, "I want Weetos for my breakfast! Now!"

My pulse galloped at the thought of the punishment I'd get. But it would all be worth it, I reminded myself. I continued screaming and stamping my feet until Mum appeared bleary-eyed at her bedroom door.

"What's all the noise?" she asked. "You need to get ready for school."

"Not going!" I shouted, elated by own defiance.

Drunk on rebellion, I marched back inside my bedroom

and slammed the door, before turning the TV up to the loudest volume. It was ear-splittingly loud; I had to put my head under my pillow to muffle the noise. Any minute, I expected someone to come in and force me to get dressed and go to school. But nobody did.

Later, I heard the taxi beeping outside, before eventually driving away without me. I felt a guilty pang as I imagined my absent mark in the register. Would Mum see it? Would she wonder where I was? Surely, she would worry. But my shame petered out into boredom as the hours passed. I risked running downstairs for some snacks when the coast was clear, before holing up once again in my bedroom. It wasn't until later in the afternoon, when the smell of fried bacon wafted upstairs, that Karl ordered me down into the living room.

"Come and eat your tea!" he shouted.

"I will not!" I yelled rebelliously. "I want chocolate spread on toast or I'm not coming out."

I thought I heard him sniggering, but I couldn't be sure. I braced myself for punishment. But nothing happened. They left me alone all night and their disinterest, in many ways, hurt more than a thwack from Ray's belt.

My empty belly growled and protested as I tried to sleep that night. But I assured myself it would all work out in the end. Their silence was surely a sign that they'd had enough of me.

The next day, when I arrived home from school, the social worker's car was parked outside. Inside, I whooped in celebration. I felt like punching the air and skipping down the path. You did it Stace! You're going home! The house was unusually quiet when I walked in. But if that was a warning, I was too blinkered to recognise it. Already I was planning how I would round up all my friends when I got home and organise a big game of football. I'd have waffles for tea. I'd play Scrabble after my bath. I was hovering in the living room doorway, anxious to start packing, when the social worker said, "These first few weeks seem to have gone well. And so we'll make it a permanent move."

My legs wobbled, as if they might give way completely.

Sheffield Wednesday — that's it. they were the third team to be relegated…

"…with visits to the Robinsons every fortnight…"

Chelsea won the FA cup

"But this is now your home, Stace…"

1-0 — was it Di Matteo who scored? Was it? Was it?

Panic bubbled in my throat like bile. Turning, I ran. Ran from the house, from the street, from the nightmare.

How had they got this so wrong? I was not wanted here. I was not loved here. I needed to go home! Every plan I made seemed to disintegrate and instead trigger the opposite reaction. My best behaviour at home had led to me being taken away. My worst behaviour here had led to me staying permanently. And even as I ran, and my lungs burned, I knew I would at some point have to turn around and go back. I had no other choice. The decision was made, and my opinion counted for nothing.

That Friday, I was allowed an overnight visit home. Better still, I was told I could go home with my foster mum after school, just like the old days. As I walked into the hallway and hung my bag on the coat hook, I felt the doors and walls sagging with relief.

Here she is! Back where she belongs!

I was in the house only moments before a cluster of my friends gathered on the path outside.

"Are you playing out, Stace?" they asked. "Have you got your boots? Are you going to be striker?"

"Just try and stop me!" I beamed.

There was a catharsis in that first visit, as though the house, the street itself, recognised me, absorbed my sadness, and relieved me of it. I had passed my burden on, and I felt lighter for it. Out on the field, I scored goal after goal. The wind on my face was revitalising and I felt sharper and faster than I'd ever been.

Mum had toasted waffles waiting when I went back inside, and Dad had set up a game of Scrabble. It was everything I had dreamed of. I could almost believe the previous few weeks had been a nightmare or a terrible mistake. I had been plonked into someone else's life in error and now, like the little figure in the dolls' house, I was back where I belonged!

That night, before bed, I climbed into the wardrobe for old times' sake, and smiled to myself. I was not hiding from anyone or anything. I just loved the nostalgia of being here. But that was the problem with nostalgia, it was a desire to return to the past, and the past had gone. And the next morning, when Dad checked his watch, my world fell apart once again.

"Time to go, Stace," he said.

Driving away, saying goodbye all over again, was like

ripping the scabs off old wounds. I could not go through it again. My heart ached with sadness as I watched the house grow smaller and smaller in the wing mirror. The pyramid of sand in the park had almost completely vanished, dug up and washed away, save for a small, sad pile.

* * * *

The contrast between the two houses, and the two families, only made the transition more painful. Being fussed over and spoiled once a fortnight made it so much harder to readjust to the apathy at my new house. I was constantly having to remind myself of two standards of behaviour and two ways of being. And, also, of two mothers.

At my foster home, there was rarely a raised voice or a cross word. But the mood in my new house was volatile. When Karl's friends were in a bad mood, they were likely to lash out with a crack across the back of my head, or even a whack with a belt. Bizarrely, when he was in good humour, Karl would stand by the window and clap slowly and ominously, as if counting down to some unknown horror. I found his clapping even more menacing than his temper. Towards the end of my final term at primary school, I remembered my foster mother's birthday was coming up.

"Could I buy her a present?" I asked Mum. "Just something small. Please?"

I had £16 in savings, money from birthdays and Christmases past, so I needed nothing more than her permission.

Even so, as I heard her consulting with Karl, I expected them to say no. To my surprise, he said, "Yeah okay, we'll go to the shop later and you can get a card and a box of chocolates."

I was thrilled. We'd always made such a fuss of birthdays back home, and I'd been saddened at the thought of letting it pass by. I knew what it was like to be forgotten and I didn't want my foster mum to feel that way too. But when we got home, with the birthday card, Mum said, "Write it out now: 'To Grandma, from Stace.'"

My gaze flickered from her to Karl in confusion.

"Grandma?" I questioned.

"She's your Mum," Karl said impatiently nodding his head towards my mother. "You've only got one. Either you write Grandma, or you don't write it at all."

I could not articulate why or how it was wrong. I just knew my heart was hurting. And as I wrote the message, I understood it would hurt my foster mother, too. The next day in school as she read my card, she swallowed hard, and her face fell.

"Thanks, Stace," she stuttered.

Soon after, under my coat hook, I found a packed lunch wrapped in a clear plastic bag. At first, I thought it belonged to someone else, but then I spotted a mini packet of Jaffa cakes, a yoghurt in a small separate bag, and a white bread chocolate sandwich. My heart filled with happiness. This was exactly the same as my packed lunches of old, and I knew it had been prepared by one person only. There was no note. No explanation. And when I saw my foster mother, later that morning, she made no reference to it. But the knowledge she had done something especially for me made every bone in my body smile. Even the Jaffa cakes seemed to wink conspiratorially when the lunch bell rang. I polished off every crumb, enjoying my lunch all the more because it was prepared with love.

From then, there was a packed lunch waiting under my coat hook every morning. No words. No secret smiles. Those lunches were a token of my foster mother's devotion and for me, they were about so much more than food. As an adult, I now understand that I was a pawn, much of the time. I was collateral damage, caught up in the bad feeling between the two families following a court's decision for me to live with my mother.

My foster mother's birthday was simply an opportunity to hurt her and me, and the birthday card was nothing but an act of spite. Every day at school I wanted to apologise to her, to explain I had been forced to write it. But I was too afraid in case I made things worse. On my next visit home, I ran upstairs, and found the bunkbeds had been replaced by one single bed, which belonged to Donna.

"Where am I sleeping?" I asked, my face crumpling.

Donna showed me a foldaway bed, in my parents' bedroom.

"It made sense. You're only here every two weeks…" she faltered.

It was like a dagger right through me.

That afternoon, when my friends invited me out to play, I shook my head. Instead, I sat in the living room and brooded. I stiffened as I heard their shrieks of laughter, their whoops of celebration as a goal was scored. Once, I'd been at the heart of that group. I'd slotted in perfectly. Now, I no longer had a place. It felt like a farce, coming here, every two weeks, pretending I was one of them. A swell of bitterness rose like acid in my throat when I thought of them going home after football to their parents and their siblings. Why couldn't I have that? Why couldn't I belong here, as they did in their homes?

There were fewer photos in the house now, I noticed. But there was still a small selection capturing me at various stages of my childhood. Happy times – all erased. I didn't even have a bed here. I did not belong here in Stockport, and I did not belong in Oldham. Flitting from nest to nest, I was a little cuckoo without a home.

9

FOR THE final day of primary school I had been invited to my foster parents' house, because the rest of my classmates were planning to camp out in celebration. A huge game of football was planned, followed by a barbeque and a few tents on the patch of grass opposite the houses.

"Can I go? Can I go?" I asked Mum.

She looked to Karl, who said, "Yeah, you can go. But that's the last time, and make sure you let them know that."

His words whipped right through me. No matter how uncomfortable I now felt at the Robinsons, I still called it home, and the idea I might never see them again was unthinkable.

Come on, Stace, I said to myself. *You have to say something. You have to.*

Manchester United won Intercontinental Cup. First time ever! Who did they beat? Can't remember… Begins with a P…

And then, it came rushing out in one breath, like a gust of wind.

"Karl. Mum. Please. I need to see them. They're my mum

and dad. I want to move back. I don't want to live here. Sorry. I'm sorry. Please let me go."

Palmeiras!

Mum stared firmly into the middle distance, focussing on the wall behind me. Karl snorted derisively.

"That's the last time. And that's final," he said. "Don't ask again."

Again, I thought of the sand mountain. Again, I felt like I was sinking.

On our last day in year six, we performed a pantomime for the rest of the school. Afterwards, we had a party where we danced, and my friends showed off their rapping skills. But the best moment came when the headteacher, whose hair had been the subject of debate for the past seven years, suddenly whipped off his wig with a flourish, to reveal a shiny bald head underneath.

"I knew it! I knew it!" we all yelled.

There were emotional tears all round as we said our goodbyes, but the mood was buoyant and excited. It wasn't until I arrived home, with my foster Mum, that Karl's words forced their way up to the front of my mind.

That's the last time, and make sure you let them know that.

It felt as though someone had smacked the joy right out of me. How could I camp out, knowing that this was the end? How could I tell my parents I would never see them again? When it came time to gather outside with our sleeping bags and bed rolls, I began to feel nauseous. I hovered around the kitchen door, unsure how to attract my foster mother's attention. I was too afraid to call her Mum, in case my other mother and Karl found out somehow. I could not bring myself to call her Grandma. That was just absurd. And 'Mrs Robinson' was simply too formal. Instead, I stood there, shifting uneasily from one foot to the other, until she turned from the sink.

"Ooh, Stace you gave me a fright there! What's the matter, pet?"

"I'm really not feeling well," I said quietly. "I think I'll stay in and just have a cheesy pizza please. I don't want to camp."

"Okay," she said, and continued with her chores around the kitchen. Seeing her perform her daily tasks brought a lump to my throat. She sprayed the draining board and worktops with cleaner, shook out the dishcloth and folded it neatly into four, then hung her rubber gloves over the tap to dry. At once mundane and precious, I wished this scene could last forever. I might never witness it again.

That's the last time, and make sure you let them know that.

I cleared my throat again and again, trying to work up to making the announcement. I needed to let her know this was my final visit. But I just couldn't say it. My mouth was parched. My heart was twisting. I could not say it out loud.

"Here you go, sweetheart," she said, opening the oven and sliding my pizza out onto a plate. "You might feel better when you've had this."

Blinking back tears, I took my place at the dining table. One last cheesy pizza. One last taste of happiness. One last memento of home. But I had a wedge in my throat, which made me think of the wedge against my bedroom door in Oldham, and I couldn't swallow a single morsel.

"I feel sick," I said, as my foster mum scooped it into the bin. "I'm going to bed."

The next morning, as Dad drove me back, I tried again to break the news. But my windpipe was so constricted, I could not squeeze out a single word. Worry expanded like foam, filling my skull, leaving no room for any other emotion. And when the car stopped, I ran into the house without looking back. Perhaps he thought I was delighted to be there. Maybe he presumed I couldn't wait to get away from him. It is tragic how so many of my behaviours were misinterpreted or ignored. How different things might have been if only communication had been easier, if only someone – anyone – had asked me how I really felt and where I really wanted to live!

Two weeks on, Dad came to the door once again to collect me for my usual visit. I was upstairs in my bedroom, hugging my football close to my chest. There were raised voices, and a short argument before I heard the front door close. And with it, the portal to my old life was slammed shut. I was not even allowed to return to my foster home to collect the rest of my belongings. I lost some of my toys, most of my Polly Pockets were left behind. I lost a couple of my United football shirts too. And amongst the mess, I lost myself.

* * * *

Those summer holidays before I started high school, stretched out before me like a desert, with no plans, no activities and no trips away. I was used to spending time at the caravan in Scarborough. I looked forward to trips to see Granny. I was kept busy with football, Irish dancing, and chess club. But in my new life, there was nothing planned. Nothing at all.

For anyone who doesn't play sport it might be difficult to understand. But football kept me alive during those long and intolerable days. I made friends on the street, managing to impress the local kids with my Cruyff turns and my rabonas. I could do hundreds of keepy-ups too, way more than any of the boys, who either dismissed me out of jealousy or did their best to outdo me. Football was my social currency, it was my way of connecting with other kids.

Sometimes, Mum's friends would offer to play with me in the back garden, too. Karl might take me out for an hour to the local park. But any joy I felt, whipping in free kicks, was rapidly followed by a conflicting stab of guilt. It seemed somehow wrong to feel happy, away from my foster family. It was wrong to be celebrating goals, showing off my skills, laughing with my new friends. And so mostly, I stayed on my own. From early in the morning, until dark, I was outside with my football. More than a social codebreaker, more than a way of getting out of the house, football kept me sane, and it kept me going. My football was my best friend, my glimmer of light in a bleak world. One evening after I'd been playing out, Karl and Mum told me to sit down in the living room. Inwardly, I groaned, wondering what I was in trouble for now.

"Good news!" Karl said. "But first, I've got a question for you, Stace. Do you want a brother or a sister?"

Bewildered, I said nothing.

"Well?" he pressed again, a note of irritation creeping in. "Haven't you guessed? Your mum is having a baby and you're going to get a brother or a sister. So, what would you like?"

I knew I should say something, but all I could think was that I had a sister and brothers back home. Why would I want another? Why did everyone persist in replacing what I already had? My home, my parents, and now my siblings. Each one stolen from me and replaced with a version I didn't like. The very fabric of my life had been ripped apart and torn to shreds. Karl was bubbling with annoyance, and if I wasn't in trouble before, I certainly was now.

"I don't mind," I stuttered eventually, as a fat tear rolled down my cheek. "I just don't mind."

But deep down, I longed to see my sister and brothers again. I missed them all so much, it was like a twisted form of grief, knowing they were alive but just out of reach. I did not want replacements or improved versions or understudies for the role. I just wanted them back.

I had a faint hope that with a new baby on the way, Mum might allow me to leave; a basic one-in, one-out policy. I wondered about suggesting it but was too afraid of the potential backlash. The next morning, I woke with such a longing to see my foster family that I could not stop crying. The tears fell, right through breakfast and into the afternoon. Eventually, in desperation, Mum agreed to call them.

"Your grandma will take you to the cinema this evening," she told me. "Just a one-off. Okay?"

I knew she was referring to my foster mum and I was thrilled. Again, I built myself up to the visit. Again, I dared to hope that perhaps they would let me go home for good.

Mum picked me up, we drove to the cinema, and without needing to ask, she bought me toffee popcorn and a mixed slush puppy. She knew exactly what I liked, as a mother should.

"Time to go now, Stace," she said, as the credits rolled at the end of *A Bug's Life*. "I promised I'd have you back by 8pm."

In the darkness of the auditorium, I bit back on my tears and instead, my sadness hardened into anger. Anger at her for letting me go so easily. Anger at myself that I had not yet learned to stop hoping. These little snatches at happiness did me no good. I was simply prolonging the agony, gouging the wound deeper. Yet I couldn't help it. I just kept on telling myself that things would get better. The promise was as tantalising as it was empty, and I fell for it every time. When I got home from the cinema, I ran upstairs and unpacked my certificates and rosettes from the box under the bed. There were a couple of shiny gold trophies too, from football and netball tournaments.

"One day, I will make something of myself," I said out loud. "One day, I will show them all."

I couldn't see how or when, but I was determined not to give up on myself, even though everyone else already had.

* * * *

A few days after the cinema trip, I was playing out on the street when a teenage girl, who lived a few doors away, suggested we get a bus into Oldham town centre.

"I'm not allowed," I said doubtfully.

"Oh, they'll never know," she said, swatting away my protests. "We'll be back in a couple of hours. Can you lend me the fare though?"

She was about 15, four years older than me, and so I went along with her plan. Besides, I knew she was right; Mum and Karl wouldn't even miss me. And whatever I did, I got into trouble. The way I saw it, life couldn't get much bleaker.

"Meet you at the bus stop in five minutes," I said, and I ran inside to get my savings to pay for us both. But we had only just got off the bus in town when she said, "Right, you're on your own now. I'm going to meet some mates. You'll have to find your own way back."

Whilst processing the shock, I was eyeing up the opportunity. I wasn't far from the train station. How hard could it be to get back to my foster home? I imagined myself turning up on the doorstep, bedraggled and exhausted.

"Come in, Stace," my mother would say. "I'll run you a hot bath and put a jacket potato in the oven. I'll call the social worker too. I'll tell her you're staying with us."

At the very least, she might let me stay overnight. It took me an age to get a train and a bus and then walk the remainder of the route to my old home. I passed the shop, where I'd spent the stolen £10. I passed the tree, my hiding spot when I ran away. I passed the park, the place where my life had started to disintegrate. By the time I arrived at the front door, my idea, like every idea I ever had, seemed suddenly very flawed and foolish.

"Stace!" my foster mother shrieked. "What are you doing here? Goodness, you will be in so much trouble! Come on in. We need to let Lisa know where you are."

I knew, right then, yet another plan was shattered. I waited in the hallway whilst she called my mother. As I listened to the conversation, my mind boggled and my head throbbed. My mother was calling my mother, from my home, arranging to take me home. It was no wonder I felt disorientated.

"I'll drive you back now," she said, ending the call. "And really Stace, you must not do this again. It's dangerous."

Mum and Karl were furious when I got back to Oldham, and I was sent straight to bed. Later, when their friends arrived, I heard Ray on the landing, outside my room, "Oi! Weird kid! Are you in there or have you run away again?"

He laughed softly to himself, and I buried my head under my pillow to block out his taunts. I remembered my trophies and my certificates under my bed and I reminded myself I must not give up.

Into August, Mum gave up her work as a cleaner to prepare for the baby coming. As her bump grew, so did my affection and enthusiasm. I loved babies, and I reminded myself I could love this one, as well as my siblings back home. I did not have to make a binary choice.

"Can I feel your tummy?" I asked her, gently placing my hand on her belly. "Ooh, I can feel him kicking. See that? Was it a hiccup?"

I couldn't wait for the baby to arrive. Yet though I was bonding with this new life, my relationship with my mother had stagnated. Day to day, she carried out perfunctory tasks such as washing and ironing. I always had clean bedding and the house was generally tidy. Her friends cooked, and though I didn't like the food, there was always something on offer. But these tasks required no input from me, and we existed in parallel, with no crossover.

Mum did not ask about my homework, or my friends, and she had no interest in football. There were no girly chats, no giggles, no sharing of lipsticks or trips out to buy a first bra. Having been at the hub of a loving family, with a mother hen who clucked over me, I felt the lack so keenly. One afternoon, my maternal granddad and his partner called to see us, bringing with them a stack of old-fashioned jigsaws; bargains from a mooch around the charity shops in the town centre.

"I know how much you love a jigsaw, Lisa," my granddad said, and I felt a ripple of surprise.

I was a big fan of jigsaws myself. After they'd gone, I suggested, "Shall we have a go at this 200-piece, the one with the horses on the picture?"

My mother smiled and we settled down on the sofa together, turning over all the pieces, slotting in the corners and the sides. It was the only thing we'd ever done together, and I loved it. I enjoyed the synchronicity of jigsaws; each piece having its own place. I only wished my only life was that straightforward. And even then, aged 11, I felt sorry for my mother. Just as I was missing out on her as a mum, she was missing out on having me as a daughter.

****

Late in the summer, just before I started at high school, Mum announced we were going camping along with a couple of families from our street. I'd never been camping before, and I was really excited. More than that, I felt she was making an effort for my sake. Aside from painting my room, and completing a few jigsaws, she hadn't ever done anything outside of the ordinary for me.

The camping trip, to the Derbyshire hills, was both a success and disaster. The weather had been hot and sticky in the days before we left and the night we arrived, the weather broke. Cowering in a tent during a thunderstorm was as exhilarating as it was frightening. The others suggested we could play memory games to distract ourselves: "I went to the shop and I bought – an antelope, a boat, a camera, a dress, an elephant…"

All too soon it was my turn.

"Stace?" prompted one of the campers.

"A family," I blurted out, much louder than I had intended.

And the tent went silent. Art imitating life. The cruel joke was, I already had two families. Yet tragically, neither had me. My breath caught in my throat as Karl's eyes met mine in the orange-tinted tent light. Thankfully, the game moved on.

"Glue, Hippo, Ink…"

And I hoped my faux pas was forgotten.

As the storm intensified, I wondered whether my own anxiety was aggravating the storm, if the weather was at the source of the problem, or was it me? With each clap of thunder, each flash of lightning across the flimsy canvas, I let out a little yelp of fear.

"It's okay, Stace," Mum murmured, pressing me close to her. "It's okay."

She radiated warmth from her baby bump, and I interpreted that as comfort and snuggled into her. This was, I realised, the closest we had ever been. Perhaps she felt, within the unique environment of the tent, she could be herself. None of her and Karl's so-called friends were sitting in judgement. Maybe, like me, she was scared too. She was not generally affectionate or tactile and for my part, I was very guarded and standoffish. Often, I felt as though I had an invisible electric fence around me. *Do not approach! Trespassers will be electrocuted!* I did not want her to love me, because I already had a mum who had loved me and look how that had turned out. Only in the gloom of the tent, as the storm raged, did I allow my defences to crumble just a little.

"Listen, here's the rain," Mum said, tipping her head slightly. "That means the storm is nearly over."

When we got home, there was only a week to go until the start of high school. I had no uniform, no shoes or bag, and this was just another worry to add to my neuroses. The day before the new term, a grant finally landed and Mum took me to a uniform shop to pick out a white shirt, blue and white tie, black blazer and black trousers. I was so slight and skinny that even the smallest sizes hung off me like drapes.

"It will have to do," the assistant sighed. "We've nothing else."

And the grant, it seemed, did not extend to shoes and coats. The grant, it seemed, did not care one bit whether I was warm or dry. In the end, Mum bought me the cheapest of each that she could find.

Through the lens of bitter experience, I can appreciate this was probably all she could afford. I am a single mother myself now and I understand all too well how hard it is to budget and to make money last. But this was about so much more than cash. There were other, equally cheap shoes and coats which would have been less demeaning to wear. The coat, in particular, a pathetic imitation of a bubble coat with all bubbles deflated, was an embarrassment. It felt, as I zipped it up, like a mood metaphor. The bubbles sagged and drooped as if they themselves were disappointed with the overall aesthetic. And the shoes, black, plastic and a size too big, were horrible. My steps dragged and I was barely able to keep them on my feet. The grant, it seemed, did not care one bit whether I was a laughing stock amongst my peers.

And once she had bought me the coat and shoes, my mother's work was done.

"I need pens and pencils," I told her. "I don't have a ruler or a rubber. I might need a calculator. What about a bag?"

I was allowed to pick out a cheap rucksack, and I managed to find my old pencilcase from primary school. But that was all. Already, I was marked out as different and deprived. And I hadn't even started school yet.

But possibly the biggest of all these challenges was my personal hygiene. On a whim, I had dyed my hair blue, but it was almost navy in colour and did not suit me at all. I had stopped taking care of myself, stopped bathing regularly, in the hope that someone might notice me. Nobody did – until my first day at high school.

"Eww! Look at her coat! I'm not sitting next to her."

"When did you last wash your manky hair you manky cow? And what colour is that supposed to be?"

"And why are you so skinny? Eh, Twig?"

I kept my head down, staring sullenly at my awful shoes, wishing they would all leave me alone.

In registration, our first class of the day, I found myself sitting on my own. I told myself it didn't bother me; I didn't relish the idea of meeting new pals and explaining how I'd lost my family, and I was living with strangers who didn't even like having me around.

For an 11-year-old girl, that felt deeply shameful, and I wanted to keep it to myself. I was better off alone. Yet in the back of my mind, I remembered the high school induction day, when the most popular girl in the entire year had insisted that I sat next to her. How had I gone from that to this? I'd become a social pariah since leaving my foster family.

I plucked out another memory, aged six, when Mum was working late in the office. I'd come across the Irish dancing class in the school hall and sauntered in, joining the end of the line without even waiting for an invite. Filled with enthusiasm and confidence, I was a part of everything, and I was loved by everyone. Or so I had thought. My life since then had not simply declined. It had fallen off a vertical cliff edge and I was plummeting towards certain disaster.

Even scarier, I was still falling. And my landing, when it came, would be brutal.

10

IT WAS the last lesson of the day, IT, and I was concentrating hard on the computer screen in front of me.

"Stace?" my teacher said. "You need to go to the office after the bell. There's a message from your grandparents."

I had so many sets of grandparents, I had no idea what it might be. But as I got to the door of the office, I spotted Mum's dad, his face white and drawn.

"I'm sorry, Stace," he said. "Your mum had the baby, but it was too soon, and he didn't make it. He was stillborn."

It was such a shock. I hadn't for a moment considered anything might go wrong. As we drove to the hospital, I remembered his hiccups in the womb and the way he had kicked against my hand. I couldn't believe he was gone.

Mum was in a private room, cradling the baby, who she had named Billy.

"Do you want to hold him?" she asked.

My first response was to step back. I had never seen a dead person, let alone a dead baby, and I was unnerved. Yet at the same time, I longed to cuddle him and hold him close and tell him how much I had looked forward to being his big sister.

"No, thank you," I whispered eventually.

For a couple of days, I stayed with my grandfather, but when I was too noisy, he lost patience.

"You'll have to go," he said. "You can't stay here any longer."

I was packed off to stay with Mum's friend. It was, in the context of my rollercoaster of rejections, an almost negligible snub. Yet it was further reinforcement that in order to be loved, I must first behave well. I knew how quickly I could be disposed of when I became inconvenient.

Mum came home from hospital, bringing baby Billy with her to spend a night in his home before the funeral. The tiny white coffin was open and again and again, I tried to pluck up courage to hold his hand, cuddle him and kiss him goodbye. But I could not. Paralysed by a mixture of grief and fear, I skirted around his coffin as though it was electrified. I felt his loss so deeply but I could not show it. In the weeks after the funeral, I thought back to my reaction when Karl first announced the pregnancy.

I had a sister and brothers back home. Why would I want another?

Was it my fault he had died, because I hadn't wanted him enough? I remembered again the sand mountain in the park. I had set this whole chain of events in motion by breaking the rules and going to the park that day. I had lost everything, and it was my own fault. No wonder nobody wanted me.

"I'm sorry, Billy," I whispered as the tears flowed. "I'm sorry I let you down."

* * * *

School improved a little when, after half-term, we played football in PE.

"Well that was a revelation," the teacher said as we filed off the pitch. "You're a great player and you're on the school team. We've a match next week. You're first on my team sheet."

I wanted to shrug it off and look cool, but I couldn't hide my smile. I was on the team! I was on the team! I was bursting to tell someone – but who? I hadn't seen my foster mother since the cinema trip. And nobody else would be in the slightest bit interested. But even that couldn't dim my excitement. Walking out of the changing rooms, the teacher's voice caught up with me: "Remember your boots and shin pads next week Stace! We're playing on grass."

As quickly as my heart had soared, it sank. I had a pair of tiny shin pads in the box under my bed, bought for me at primary school. But my football boots were way too small, I couldn't even get my feet inside. I'd been playing football in old trainers for the past few months. It was pointless asking Mum to get me a new pair, she was still holding out on buying me a pencilcase and pens. At the start of every lesson, I had to ask the teacher if I could borrow whatever stationery was required. It was bad enough that I was marginalised by my clothes, my hygiene, my lack of equipment. My lack of family. And now, with my big chance on the horizon, I had no football boots.

The worry gnawed at me all day and kept me awake that

night too. In the early hours, racked with anxiety, I sat up in bed and peered out of my lime-coloured curtains, onto the empty street below. More than anything, I wanted to be on the football team. I missed football like I might miss a best friend and I was desperate to play regularly. But how, without boots? I looked out, into the sky, and remembered how high I'd flown with the love of my foster parents beneath me. Living here, my wings weren't just clipped. They were broken, snapped into pieces and stamped upon. Would I ever fly again?

The day before the match, the PE teacher stopped me in the corridor.

"All set for tomorrow, Stace?" he asked. "Remember your boots. No metal studs. I'm looking forward to having you on the team."

"Sir," I said awkwardly. "I'm sorry, I can't play. Thing is, I lost one of my football boots at the weekend and there's no time to buy a new pair. I'm sorry."

He must have known I was lying to save face and he said nothing. Instead, he showed me into the PE office, where I was greeted by a musty, sweaty smell and a big box of assorted boots in the corner.

"Find your size and take them home. And don't lose this pair," he winked.

"Sir, I won't," I gabbled. "Thank you, Sir, thank you. I won't let you down."

And I didn't. I gave it my all in every match, and I never missed a single training session. Soon I was top scorer for the team, and we were steadily making our way up the league.

Back home, in my other life, my foster mother had never

missed a single match. Here, though I invited her several times, Mum didn't attend once. She never even asked me for the results.

Girls' football was not hugely popular back then, and our success was not revered at school in the same way as the boys' achievements. But my performances were enough to break the ice and I made a couple of friends. One girl, Serena, was having a hard time at home, and without exchanging confidences, there was an implicit understanding between us.

She and I both qualified for free school meals, but she brought a packed lunch and was happy to give me her ticket. Queuing twice, I was able to get two dinners, meaning I didn't need to eat in the evenings at home. It wasn't ideal, but at least I wasn't starving. One day, as I took my place in the dinner queue for the second time, the usual bullies started.

"Poor little Stace! Can't afford shampoo! Can't afford to buy her own dinner!"

A red rash of humiliation spread across my face as I looked imploringly at Serena for support. But she was laughing along with the rest of them. I understood even then why she had switched sides, it was all about self-preservation. But it stung all the same. And there was worse to come. In the schoolyard afterwards, egged on by the crowd, she sneered, "So when are you gonna stop leeching off me and start buying your own dinners?"

I was mortified – and angry too. She had offered me her dinner tickets. She didn't even use them herself. I was being portrayed as something I was not.

"I can fight you," I said, with a bravado I did not feel.

Laughing, the other kids clustered around us, keen not to miss out on the fun.

"Come on then," she said.

I knew I was heading for certain humiliation, but I had gone too far. I couldn't back down now. Serena, who was much bigger than me, floored me with a single punch. I was so light, I almost blew away, like the empty crisp packets and drinks cans which littered the side of the yard.

"I can fight you," she mimicked sarcastically. "I can fight you."

The other kids crowded round as I lay on the concrete. Someone aimed a kick at my stomach. Someone else grabbed my bag and emptied it out on the ground.

There is an old belief that there is nowhere colder than a schoolyard and nobody crueller than school bullies. Yet though it was tough, I knew different. Going home was much, much worse.

"Alright, weirdo?" Karl asked as I slumped onto the sofa that night. "We don't want to look at your miserable face. Get to your room."

With the loss of my extra dinner ticket, I began losing weight again. I rarely ate in the evenings because I didn't like the food at home. Aged 10, I had weighed four stone. And now, approaching my 12th birthday, I still weighed four stone.

One afternoon, while playing netball in PE, I keeled over with stomach pain. Another time, in assembly, I collapsed in a heap. After the school nurse called home, Mum and Karl took me to the GP.

"She doesn't eat a thing," Karl told him. "So fussy."

I didn't speak during the entire consultation. Didn't dare. I could not have begun to explain that my eating issues were so deep-seated I didn't understand them myself. But I was sure of one thing: I was not starving myself on purpose. I physically could not swallow the food that I was given. I might just as well have had a stopper blocking my throat.

"Well," the doctor said. "She'll eat when she's hungry. Bring her back if she doesn't start putting on weight."

Afterwards, my size and shape came under the microscope more than ever. Now, when I couldn't eat my evening meal, instead of leaving me sitting at the table, Karl and his friends invented games for me instead. One night, Ray waved a scarf at me and said, "Come here, weird kid."

He wrapped it tightly around my head as a blindfold and spun me a few times.

"Now, let's see if you can find your way back to your dinner, golf club legs!"

Through my dizziness, I concentrated hard on the weekend football results.

Manchester City 0, Leeds United.

They laughed as I stumbled around the room, banging into furniture. I kept tripping over outstretched legs which seemed to appear everywhere I turned. When the tears leaked through my blindfold, they laughed all the louder.

"Hey, Twiggy!" they giggled. "You'll snap those legs if you keep falling over!"

Liverpool beat Villa away, 3-0.

They made fun of my teeth, too, which stuck out a little.

"Come on Goofy! See if you can squeeze some dinner past those big teeth, Bugs Bunny!"

Everton v Spurs, 0-0.

Even though I couldn't see her, I knew Mum was there, watching. I could hear her whimpering, every now and again. But she did not speak up for me. She didn't even help me up when I fell over. She had been quieter than ever since losing Billy and my heart bled when I thought of what she had lost. But that didn't excuse her deserting me when I needed her the most and resentment crackled through me like an electric current.

Their heartless games continued, and I became petrified of mealtimes. The smell of cooking sent me into paroxysms of panic and sitting at the dining table was like taking my place in a firing squad. Back at the GP surgery, the doctor told me sternly that I was becoming anorexic, and I would either have to eat or go into hospital.

"This is a serious situation," he told us.

But then, I already knew that. My problem was how to escape it.

11

ON MY 12th birthday, in April 2001, it was impossible not to think of my old life, of the birthday cakes, the parties, the over-indulgent gifts. I wanted to forget about my foster family, to wipe them clean from my mind. Yet at the same time, I savoured each memory and longed to be back there. I hated and adored them, missed them and despised them, all at once. My foster parents no longer held my hand each day, but I knew they would always hold my heart. Soon after my birthday, I was selected to play in a prestigious tournament with the school football team.

"Stace, I'm counting on you," my teacher said. "This is a big deal."

I beamed, pleased by the responsibility. The rest of my life might be in ruins around me, but I was always confident on the football field.

The tournament was being held at a school across town and we would travel there and back by minibus. Many parents and other pupils were coming along too in support. Mum knew about it, but wasn't coming to watch.

The big day dawned and on the minibus I felt that familiar cocktail of excitement and nerves; desperate to win, anxious not to lose. We breezed through the rounds with easy wins. But in the final, we were facing a good team and we were evenly matched. By half-time, we were 2-0 up and I had scored both goals. Then, moments into the second half, our goalkeeper came off injured. We had no substitute goalie that day, and it spelled disaster for the team.

"Sir!" I shouted. "I'll go in goal! I've done it before!"

It was a dramatic change, from striker to goalie. But I'd had lots of goalkeeper training at primary school, and I felt sure I could do it. Pulling on the gloves, I took my place in the net and didn't concede a single goal. In the final minute, I made a vital save, my heart in my mouth as I dived full length to grab the ball. When the final whistle went, I was mobbed. The team, and all the kids who had come to watch, ran to congratulate me.

"Our match hero," smiled the PE teacher. "Well done, Stace."

As we posed for photos with our trophies, it felt like a turning point. Everyone loved me. Everyone liked me. It didn't matter much that my own family wasn't there, because other parents kept slapping me on the back and shaking my hand. I belonged. I belonged – at last!

The journey back passed in a haze of euphoria and after we arrived at school, the other players disappeared one by one into waiting cars. I slipped away, through the gates and onto the main road, a little deflated that there was no one waiting there for me. Yet nothing, nothing, could dent my joy that day.

At the bus stop, I checked all my pockets before realising I'd forgotten my bus pass. I'd have to walk home. Again, it didn't really matter. It took me almost an hour, but I barely noticed. Clutching my trophy, I relived all the best moments; my two goals, my last-minute save.

And the player of the match goes to – Stace!

I'd been told there would be a special assembly at school tomorrow and the whole team would be called on stage. I'd show all the bullies. I'd make Serena sorry. This was my metamorphosis, from slug to butterfly. I'd have so many friends from now on. Pushing open the front door, I began my announcement before I was even inside.

"We won! We won!"

I waved my trophy in the air like a mascot. But as I looked from Mum to Karl, both glaring stonily, the happiness leaked out of me.

"Where have you been?" Karl snapped.

"The tournament," I began. "I told you, remember? Then I lost my bus pass, sorry, I had to walk. But we won! And I scored! I score – "

"You're grounded," Karl interrupted. "Eat that – " he nodded at the table. "And then get to bed."

Like a punctured ball, the joy hissing out of me, I took my place at the table. A plate of cold, cheesy beans stared back at me. Karl bent low, so that his mouth was in-line with my ear.

"You eat that, or else," he growled.

With my hands shaking, I spooned in the first few mouthfuls. I managed to get halfway through it before I ran upstairs to vomit. Before I got into bed, I pulled out the box which contained all my certificates and trophies. Mournfully, I laid my new trophy to rest alongside them, before pushing the box back under the bed. It was like a funeral, with all my hopes and dreams interred in that small, coffin-like box. Any confidence I had left was shattered like a smashed window.

As I climbed into bed, I vowed that this was the end. Nobody cared about me. Nobody was proud of me. And from now on, I would make absolutely sure there was nothing to be proud of.

* * * *

The next day, despite the assembly, I skipped school. Instead of sitting in lessons, I spent the day kicking a football around the park. I no longer saw the point of trying hard and behaving well. Mum and Karl never noticed me no matter what I did. I couldn't remember a single time Mum had ever praised me for anything, and the football tournament felt like the final twist of a knife. How was it I was lauded by everyone at school, yet punished at home? Surely it was their fault, not mine, that I'd been left to walk home alone in the dark.

Angrily, I took my frustrations out on the ball and kicked it as hard as I could. I almost wanted to be found out and punished for playing truant. I was itching for a showdown. But it was surprisingly easy skipping classes, so I missed the rest of the week, as well. The problem was, playing truant was boring, and when it rained there was nowhere to keep dry. Without my school dinner, I went hungry, too. Reluctantly, I went in the following Monday, but when the teacher spoke, I began shouting and banging on my desk.

"Stace, what on earth has got into you?" she asked.

But I just banged even louder. My behaviour was stupid and infantile, but it was indicative of my state of mind. I was treated with contempt, so I would behave that way too. In my immaturity, I thought my poor behaviour would be punishment for my mother. In reality, it was punishment only for me. I was sent out of lesson several times that week, which to me seemed all too convenient a solution. And so, I began refusing to leave. When I was ordered out of the classroom, I would simply bang on the desk and holler at the top of my voice.

In music, where we had electric keyboards, I turned mine up to full volume, pretending to be the resident DJ. Everyone laughed and cheered, and this was the validation I craved. I did not see, or did not want to see, that they were laughing at me, not with me. In science, the teacher had a rule that we were not allowed to wear coats in his lesson. With this in mind, I zipped up my coat and ducked under his arm into class before he could stop me.

"Come back," he ordered.

But I planted myself firmly in my chair and I refused to move. Unsure of what to do, he evacuated the whole class, leaving me in there on my own. Just as the last pupil left, I opened the ground-floor window and jumped out, rolling onto the grass below. I sprinted across the field and out onto the road, laughing to myself as though it was all one big joke.

My teachers could not cope with me, and I relished that. I loved the notoriety. Now, at last, I was being noticed. But if there were calls home to complain, I never found out about them. Mum never raised the issue of my behaviour. What more could I do to get her attention? Parents' evening came and went, and she did not attend. It passed her by, just like everything else. Meanwhile, my behaviour spiralled further. I began standing on desks, yelling and causing a nuisance, and I was told I would be taught in isolation until my behaviour improved.

"You're not allowed to represent the school any longer," the Deputy Head informed me. "No more football matches, no more tournaments."

It was a low blow, but I could hardly blame them. It was no more than I deserved, and I was past caring anyway. I thought of the trophies in the sealed box under my bed. They were nothing more than cruel reminders of what might have been, dusty relics of another life. I realised how foolish I had been to think I could make something of myself. I was worthless. Nobody wanted me. Not my foster parents. Not my real parents. Not even my football team.

"I'll play on my own," I replied stubbornly. "I'm used to it."

The new friendships I had made after the tournament evaporated as quickly as they had formed. And that dizzy high, that feeling of floating on cloud nine, had scudded away, just as clouds do. I knew then, it would never be replicated. Though I would never have admitted it, I was searching, always, for the happiness I'd felt with my foster family. Yet it was a happiness built on lies, built on sand. How could I recreate a feeling which had never truly existed?

At home, I was less rebellious, partly because I was frightened of Karl's friends and partly because there were not many rules to push against. The main point of contention was mealtimes and, as the months passed, the GP's prediction of an eating disorder became a self-fulfilling prophecy. I started making myself sick. With a small click of my throat I found I could efficiently vomit back whatever I had eaten. Seeing my dinner floating in the toilet bowl gave me an overwhelming feeling of relief. At last, I had some control. At last, it was my decision whether or not I ate. I'd make myself sick even when my stomach was empty, retching painful splatters of green bile into the bowl. My stomach cramped and my throat throbbed with the strain. And yet, it gave me a strange sense of solace.

Despite vomiting most days, nobody noticed at home, or if they did, they never challenged me. But that just reinforced my belief that I was without worth. I deserved to be punished. My eating disorder was about control, but it was also about retribution. Food was, and always would be, linked to suffering and punishment.

Karl's friends were always eager to dole out their own punishments too. One evening I came home after dark, and they insisted I empty my pockets. In my jogging bottoms, I had one single cigarette. The irony was, I only carried it because I thought it was a way of being accepted into the local gang, who were older than me and all smoked. I had never actually smoked myself.

"See this?" Ray said, laying the crumpled cigarette on the table. "Eat it."

"What?" I replied shakily.

"Don't get smart. You heard me. You think you're so clever smoking, so you can eat it instead. Go on!"

Mum, as was her way, blended seamlessly into the furniture. With Ray towering over me, I had no choice but to do as he said. The tobacco was dry as parchment in my mouth, and he would not allow me a drink to wash it down.

"Eat it! Eat it! Eat it!" he yelled, as though he was bear-baiting.

Charlton 0, Liverpool 4. Everton 2, Sunderland 2. Newcastle beat Villa, was it 3-0? Can't remember.

Gagging, I forced down the last strands of tobacco and dashed to the bathroom. For the next hour, I continued retching and vomiting. There was nothing left in my stomach and yet still I heaved. I felt so ill. And so desperate. Then, I heard Deano's voice downstairs.

"Oi, weirdo! We got your favourite from the chippy, half chips, half rice. Cheer you up a bit."

Maybe they had panicked at going too far and they bought the chips as a woefully inadequate peace-offering. Or maybe it was all part of their game. Whatever, I couldn't eat a thing; my mouth and stomach were so sore. Even so, I dragged myself downstairs to thank them. I could not risk making them angry again.

"Oh, that was funny," Ray smirked, as I picked at my rice. "You went green eating that cig, absolutely green!"

He and Deano laughed and laughed. My mother did not

laugh, but neither did she cry on my behalf. With a big effort, I stretched my face into a sad smile, but I didn't get the joke.

* * * *

One afternoon, I came home from school to find Deano pacing the living room in a rage.

"I left my wallet here last night with £120 in it," he said. "This morning, after you went to school, it had gone. It's not rocket science. So where is it, Twiggy?"

I hadn't seen his wallet. I certainly hadn't taken his money.

"No idea," I replied.

The accusations and denials went back and forth for a few moments, before he unbuckled his belt.

"You might remember now," he said, and thwacked the back of my legs.

I had a school skirt on and the leather on my bare skin burned.

"I don't know," I sobbed. "Please leave me alone. I really don't know."

He hit me again and again, until my knees wobbled and threatened to give way. Eventually, with my legs red and swollen, he marched off to shout at Mum instead. I crawled upstairs and into bed, glaring at my David Beckham book as I eased the duvet carefully over the red marks on my skin.

"I don't know what you've got to smile about," I muttered, through my tears.

Exhausted by crying, I drifted off to sleep. My dreams were peppered with sunlit memories of cheesy pizzas, Irish dancing and trips to Scarborough, images of my old wardrobe and my old happiness. Aged seven was the last time I had felt truly safe. Would I ever feel safe again? I missed them all so much and wished I could see them, just for a moment. So it felt a little like a premonition when, the following week, Donna turned up outside school.

"I dreamed of you the other night," I told her. "I wish I could come back home."

"Me too, Stace," she said. "I've been working in Oldham, so I thought I'd come and say hello. How's it going with your Mum?"

I was bursting to tell her. Desperate to confide in her. But for some reason, I just shrugged and said, "Yeah, you know, it's fine."

Maybe I just didn't know where to start. Perhaps the indifference at home was catching, and I thought I was a lost cause. Donna took me to the bus station cafe for a hot chocolate, but as the back of my leg touched the plastic chair I winced, and she insisted on lifting my skirt.

"My god, Stace, where did you get those bruises?" she gasped.

When I began to cry, she took my hands in hers.

"You have to report this," she said. "When you go to school tomorrow, tell the teacher. Something should be done."

The next day, with Donna's advice ringing in my ears, I went to find my form teacher. Floating around the edge of my mind was also the suggestion that maybe, when the authorities realised what was happening, I'd be allowed back home to the Robinsons. The mere possibility of change was enough to outweigh the unease I felt at making the report.

"You did the right thing," my teacher told me. "I'll speak to social services today."

I was dreading going home, preparing myself for a nuclear meltdown from Karl and his friends. Perversely, I felt guilty myself. I felt I'd let Mum down, by speaking to the teachers behind her back. It breaks my heart to look back at my 12-year-old self and see the total lack of self-esteem. But nothing was said that day, or the next. Almost three weeks later, Mum said, "You have a hospital appointment about those bruises on your legs. I'll take you after school."

Deano's lip curled and he said, "Apparently someone hit you? You lying little cow. So where are your bruises?"

Three weeks on, the bruises had healed. And at the hospital, when the social worker asked me to point out my injuries, I could only hang my head.

"They're better now," I said feebly.

Social services took no further action. Deano and Ray laughed when I arrived home and as usual, the joke was on me.

Despite my vow after the tournament, a part of me still wanted to make Mum proud. I couldn't help myself. Intermittently, she gave me £1 weekly pocket money and I'd also sometimes get to keep the change if I nipped to the shop for her or her friends. We had a kind neighbour, too, named Lara, who occasionally gave me bags of spare coppers to spend.

"Treat yourself, love," she smiled.

But as I counted out the two and one pence pieces into

piles, I knew I would not spend them on myself. When I had enough money, I went to our local Post Office which had a gift shop attached and sold animal ornaments made from frosted glass. After ages of careful deliberation, I chose a glass polar bear, and took it home for Mum. If I could not get her to love me for myself, perhaps I could buy her affection instead? My heart quickened with expectation as she unwrapped the tissue paper. I felt sure this would do the trick.

"Oh, thanks Stace," she said, popping it on the end of the fireplace and disappearing into the kitchen to put the wrapping in the bin. And that was it. I felt as though I'd been pierced through my side and the air was slowly hissing out. And yet, the next time I got some money, I went straight back to the Post Office. This time, I chose a cute glass owl. Mum placed him next to the polar bear with a vague:

"Um, thanks Stace," and I was swamped with despair.

What more could I do? But there I was, a couple of months later, back in the shop, choosing a little kitten. Even as the assistant wrapped it up, the kitten stared with glassy eyes, mocking my stupidity.

This won't work Stace! You can't win your mother over with ornaments.

But I didn't know what else to do. As each glass ornament took its place on the fireplace, I felt smaller and smaller. I just kept going back for more pain; ripping off the scabs, making myself bleed, over and over again.

* * * *

One morning, in the summer holidays, there was a knock at the door and even from my bedroom, I recognised his voice immediately. Nigel Taylor, my biological father.

"Hiya Lou-Lou," he said, as I peered over the bannister. "I've come to take you out. Get your shoes on. We're going to Blackpool."

I was not at all sure about going anywhere with this man. His black eyes seemed to flash like warning lights. *Stay away!* And the long yellow hairs curling out of his nose turned my stomach. I felt slightly nauseous just looking at him.

"Come on," he said impatiently. "My girlfriend's in the car."

It was, I told myself, preferable to staying here with Mum. And his girlfriend, Sandra, turned out to be quite nice. She chatted away as we drove up the motorway and bought me an ice-cream as we wandered along the promenade. We even went on a few rides on the pleasure beach. Nigel kept a few paces ahead of us, marching with purpose, as though he was angry. Every time I saw him he seemed furious, and I wondered whether that was my fault too, like everything else.

"Have you had a good time?" he asked as he dropped me off later in the evening.

I nodded.

"Thank you… Dad," I said.

Again, the blockage in my throat, again, the surge of shame. The word felt wrong. That name belonged to my foster father. Just as Mum belonged to my foster mother. But this was just how it was now, and I had to try to move on. Strangely, my birth parents, though separated, seemed to be good friends. Mum had been 18 when I was born, Dad three years older. But they had split by the time I was two years old. Dad became a regular visitor at the house, and they seemed to get on well.

"Why did you split up, when you like him so much?" I asked Mum.

"Well, he wasn't very nice to me when you were a baby," she told me. "And when I was pregnant, he used to make me walk all the way to hospital, for my ante-natal checks. He wouldn't take me in the car, and I wasn't allowed to get the bus.

"And if the baby was a girl, he threatened to drop me over the bannister."

Bewildered, I stared at her. Did she think so little of herself that she would be friends with a man who had treated her like that?

And did she think so little of me that she would let him befriend me, too?

12

FOR MY 13th birthday, Dad bought me a blue Reebok coat, which I loved. I hadn't had a nice coat since leaving my foster family and I couldn't wait to show it off. Mum bought me eyeshadows.

Again, on my birthday, my thoughts turned to my foster family. They had not even sent me a card; had they forgotten about me completely? The idea that they could simply brush me aside was unbearable.

My frustration and sadness crystallised into cold self-loathing, and I found myself outside, around the back of the house. Scrunching my eyes shut, I scraped my knuckles down the brickwork, until each one bled. There was a grim satisfaction, a perverse sort of comfort, in seeing my hands splattered with blood.

In the weeks that followed, instead of making myself sick, I began dragging my knuckles down walls. It was, somehow, a more complete and comprehensive pain.

For Christmas that year, Dad announced that his parents had paid for a trip to Florida.

"They'd like you to come as well, Lou-Lou," he said. "A chance to get to know you better."

I'd never been to Florida, and I was naturally thrilled. My grandparents had their own holiday home there but had paid for an all-inclusive hotel stay for my father, his girl-friend, and me. They had even booked tickets for all the Disneyland parks and attractions. Mum packed me off with hardly anything in my suitcase, wearing shoes that were so small my toes were rubbed red raw.

"Oh, we can't have this," said my grandmother when I arrived.

She promptly took me out and bought me new shoes and several new outfits. As she flung T-shirts and shorts into her shopping basket, I had a flashback to life at the Robinsons. At last, someone was taking care of me as they once had. My new grandparents were lovely, and nothing like Dad. Just as I could not believe I was biologically related to my own parents, I could not credit that they were related to him, either.

On the flight over to Florida, I was bursting with excite-ment. But after we landed my grandparents went off to their own apartment leaving me with Dad and his partner, and I felt a little less sure of myself.

"We'll meet up for breakfast tomorrow," said my grand-father.

Our hotel room had a double bed, with a camp bed slotted in at the side for me. That first night, I lay on my camp bed reading my football magazine while Dad's partner had a shower.

"Come here, Lou-Lou," Dad said, diving onto the camp bed and almost upending the whole thing.

He began to tickle me, laughing and shrieking, but it felt somehow awkward and forced. I was too old for playfighting anyway. Dad was rough, and he shoved me hard, down the side of the bed, so that I was pressed against the wall. For a moment, I couldn't breathe.

"You're hurting me!" I gasped.

Dad yanked me back onto the bed, grabbing at my bottom, but it was momentary, and I was just glad to get my breath back.

"Get a sense of humour, Lou-Lou," he said scathingly, climbing onto his own bed.

The next morning, in the restaurant, Dad ordered cooked breakfasts for us all.

"I don't like bacon and sausage," I murmured. "Could I please just have toast?"

Dad glowered at me, and his yellow nostril hairs quivered.

"You will eat what you're told," he growled. "We should never have brought you. You'll ruin the whole holiday."

The waitress noticed my tears, and a few moments later she brought two slices of toast, chocolate pancakes, and orange juice.

"Thank you," I whispered.

I didn't say another word during breakfast, but when we went outside to the pool, Dad suddenly grabbed me, tipped me up and dangled me over the deep end.

"I can't swim!" I yelled. "Please don't."

He laughed and dropped me in. There were a few seconds

of agonising shock where I was plunged underwater, swallowing great chlorinated gulps, my lungs bursting. I thought I would drown. But then a strong hand circled my waist and dragged me upwards.

"Next time, eat your breakfast," said a voice in my ear.

Whilst I coughed and retched at the side of the pool, Dad paraded up and down, boasting he had saved my life.

"Good job I did my lifeguard training," he announced. "You never know when it will come in handy."

The holiday was divided into distinct sections, and the time I spent with my grandparents was wonderful. We saw all the sights and enjoyed the parks, and I dribbled my football everywhere I went. Though I had outgrown Disney, there was a moment of pure wonder when I spotted Jessie, from *Toy Story*, one of my childhood heroines. But my joy quickly vaporised as I remembered snuggling on the sofa with Donna and my brothers, watching the *Toy Story* films. It was a precious memory, but painful too.

For Christmas, in addition to everything else they had bought, my grandparents gave me a bracelet with my name on it and a Disney tree decoration. They were incredibly generous and kind. In front of his parents and his partner, Dad was fine with me. But on his own, he was vicious and nasty.

Whenever we were alone, he'd throw me onto the bed and order me to play-fight. I recoiled as he grabbed at my private parts and my chest, but I told myself it was accidental. And when I complained, he would squash me in between the bed and the wall until my lungs felt like they would explode. I became so nervous around him that I began biting my hand, gnawing at the skin around my knuckles.

"You little weirdo," he sneered. "Stop showing me up."

So, while the world of Disney was shiny and fun-filled, there was, for me, a dark underbelly of angst and despair. And though I dreaded going home, I hated being in Florida with Dad. Before we left, I used my savings to buy a Disney watch for Mum and a Mickey Mouse T-shirt for Karl. Maybe, I thought, as I packed them in my case, this would make them like me a little bit more.

Arriving back in Oldham, I was not expecting much of a welcome, but I could not help feeling disappointed all the same. Mum smiled when she unwrapped her watch, but Karl didn't even bother opening his gift. They had bought me nothing for Christmas. Not a single present. My impression was that they were utterly dismayed to have me back. A few days later, before the start of the new school term, Mum said, "Listen Stace, I need to talk to you. I have to choose between you and Karl…"

West Ham Fulham, 1-1 draw.

"And so, I'm afraid…"

Bolton 4, Newcastle 3.

I did not wait to hear her decision. I ran upstairs, with my hands clapped over my ears, furiously reciting football scores. Throwing my clothes into bags, I had no idea where I would even go. My foster family did not want me. And now my own mother did not want me. What had I done that was so wrong?

A little while later, Mum tapped on my door.

"You're going to live with Nigel and his girlfriend," she said. "He's on his way for you now."

I sank onto the end of the bed with my head in my hands. Every time I was alone with him, he made me cry. He was violent and cruel and twisted. And now I was going to live with him.

"Why?" I asked, in a small voice. "Why did you not pick me?"

It was like holding my hand in a fire. I knew I was going to get burned and yet I did it all the same. Mum sighed sadly.

"When you're grown up, I'll have nobody," she said. "And so I have to choose Karl."

****

If Mum's house was lacking in routine, Dad's was complete anarchy. He actively encouraged me to skip school, preferring instead that I did housework during the day, and stayed up to watch late-night wrestling on TV with him. I was a wrestling fan too, but where I had once looked for similarities between us, I now hoped to distance myself as much as possible. I did not want to be like my father at all.

It was my job to do all the cleaning, washing, and ironing. I was also expected to sweep the backyard and keep the garden tidy, a task I loved because I could take my football outside with me. Every evening, Dad's inspections of my housework were strict and regimental. He would often brag about his time in the army, although his own father had told me he'd been sent home after failing a medical and had never actually served a single day as a soldier. I knew better than to question him, instead, grinding my teeth in nervous anticipation as he ran his finger along the fireplace to check for dust, or he inspected the kitchen worksurface for crumbs.

"Lou-Lou!" he'd yell, and my heart would drop right through my legs as though they were hollow. "Did you polish the doorknocker? I can see a smear."

I was never sure whether he loved cleanliness, or he simply loved to see me cleaning. When my work was not up to standard, the punishment was always physical. I got a crack across the back of the head, or a punch to the stomach, and I soon learned the best course of action was to take it, without objection or protest, and certainly without tears. The key was not to react. Dad favoured a stiff upper lip, another legacy from his fantasy army career. On the odd occasion I was unable to hold back tears, Dad became infuriated and hit me again and again.

"If you cry, you get double," he always said.

He hated any sign of weakness or emotion, and my weeping made him even angrier than the transgression which had prompted the punishment in the first place.

"Next time," he bawled, aiming a punch at my midriff, "Don't be so soft!"

It was best just to let him hit me, as it gave him some sort of release, and he was always calmer afterwards. He signed me up with the local army cadets and if my boots weren't shining, he'd clatter me round the head with them. With my ears ringing, I just had to bite my lip and take it.

Don't cry, Stace, I told myself. *Don't cry.*

Man City 1, Birmingham 0. Liverpool beat Spurs 3-2. West Brom got beat by Chelsea, 2-0 I think…

Dad's girlfriend had a part-time job in a local shop, but she also had several health issues. Whenever she was too ill to go to work, I was expected to take her place. The cash I earned, £20 a day, had to be handed straight to Dad. I did not dare ask for a share for myself. She was admitted to hospital for a while, and one of my chores was to visit, taking her clean nightwear and underwear. I soon got to know the other patients on the ward, and I fell into a routine of taking their orders for the local shop before running the errand. Coming back, loaded down with bags of crisps, drinks, newspapers and sweets, I could not help smiling. And though I had vowed never to try to please anyone again, I felt stirrings of satisfaction as I handed out my wares. I loved to feel needed. Sadly, I could see no worth for myself, if not through the prism of how I might be useful to others.

"What would we do without you, Stace?" they asked. "You're a little gem."

In the evenings, Dad persuaded me to stay up late, watching films or wrestling. His girlfriend, when she wasn't in hospital, always went to bed early, leaving the two of us alone. At first, I sat on a chair by the door, as far away from him as I could. But Dad said, "Come on, cuddle up on the sofa here with me, Lou-Lou. Tell you what, if you come and sit here, I'll roll you a ciggie."

I felt horribly conflicted as I took my place perched on the end of the couch. Like any typical 13-year-old, part of me was quite thrilled to have a father who insisted I played truant, let me stay up late and allowed me to smoke. But, quite aside from his temper and his cruelty, something just didn't feel quite right. While I stared resolutely at the telly, I was aware of Dad's eyes fixed on me. In my pink silky pyjamas, a gift from my grandparents, I felt vulnerable and uncomfortable.

"I love your pyjamas," Dad remarked, leaning in, and rubbing his finger briefly down my leg. "Gosh, they're soft, aren't they?"

Quietly, I nodded but internally, I flinched. And while I might have been the envy of my friends, with a cool dad who let me stay up late, I would really much rather have been in bed asleep.

My 14th birthday, in April 2003, was not marked in any way. I hadn't heard from Mum since leaving in January and she didn't send me a birthday card or a present. There was nothing from my foster family, either, who might not even know where I lived. They had probably forgotten all about me anyway.

I had worked hard at cauterising my feelings; it was like playing hide and seek with my memories, dodging all the rec-ollections that broke my heart, over and over again. But on my birthday, my defences caved in, and I missed them all so much; Mum, Dad, Donna, Daniel and Paul. I remembered my seventh birthday party, the caterpillar cake, the yellow Liverpool football kit, the penalty shootout in the garden. I clung to these little starbursts of joy, for they were all I had. And although it hurt so much to look back into the past, it hurt even more to look into the future. Late at night in bed, I would unpack the box that contained my certificates and trophies, and remind myself that one day, I would make something of my life. I clung to the desperate belief that this sorrow would not last.

A few days after my birthday, Dad announced he would be away overnight.

"I want this place shipshape and clean when I get back," he said, wagging a finger in my face.

As I heard his car engine roar into life, the relief ran through me like honey. What could I do with a whole 24 hours to myself? Even before I'd finished the question, I was pulling on my coat and looking up the bus times. By early afternoon, I was trundling through Stockport looking out at all the familiar landmarks. It was surprisingly easy to get in through the school gates; everyone recognised me and welcomed me in.

"Stace!" my foster mum gasped when I poked my head around the office door. "Well, what a surprise!"

"I know! I just thought I'd pop in," I smiled, as though I'd been passing.

All through the journey, I'd been buzzing with nervous energy, but now that I was here, I couldn't think of anything to say. I was so desperate to make a good impression, so anxious for her to want me back. And yet in trying too hard, I somehow failed to try at all. There was an oppressive silence during which I racked my brains for a witty comment or a snippet of news and found nothing.

"I'd better be going," I said eventually. "I'm actually in a hurry."

"Take care," smiled my foster mum, opening her filing cabinet.

The moment I walked out of the gates, I had an almost overwhelming desire to dash back in, rectify the awkwardness, and start all over again. Why had I messed it up?

And it didn't stop there. Almost without making a conscious decision, I found myself, a few weeks later, on my way back to Stockport. The bus dropped me at an unfamiliar stop, but almost through muscle memory, I found my way to the top of my old street. It was as though I had an inbuilt sat-nav, leading me home. I positioned myself so that I could just see the front door, the bedroom window and the patch of grass where I used to play. My plan had been to knock on the door and hope they would take me back, but now that I was here, I could see how short-sighted I had been. Again. I would have to make do with waiting here instead.

With a shudder, I remembered the disturbing way my father had stood at the top of the street, waiting to ambush me as I left the house as a seven-year-old. Did this mean I was like him? The parallels were there. Maybe I shouldn't have come. But I missed it all so much, it hurt. The desire to be wrapped up once again in a warm beam of familial love was so strong it winded me. Turning, I walked back to the bus stop, tears streaming down my face. I could not keep putting myself through this, and yet I couldn't stop.

The next time I visited, some months on, there was a removal van outside, and I spotted my foster father carrying boxes out of the house. The scene was like a knife right through me. They were moving, and they hadn't even told me!

What about my bedroom, my wardrobe, my Polly Pockets? Who would wear my old football shirts? Who would have my duvet covers? I advanced a little nearer and saw Donna coming out of the door carrying binbags. The symbolism was as clear as it was callous: They were moving on, without me. I was no longer a part of the family and perhaps I never had been. Slumped on the pavement, my head resting on my knees, I watched as more of my memories were dismantled and demolished. As more of my life was discarded and junked. Eventually, there would be nothing left of me. The house windows stared down on me, blank and indifferent, and as the front door slammed, one final time, it seemed to shout:

Yeah, good riddance to you Stace! We never wanted you here!

13

THANKS TO my football skills, I made new friends on Dad's street, including a best pal, Katrina, whose brother, Sammy, was my age, and asked, very politely, if I would like to be his girlfriend. I agreed immediately and when we weren't playing football, the two of us would sit on the wall outside his house and hold hands. We never so much as kissed, but to us, we were in a serious relationship. I felt like I'd been married for 20 years the way we cheerfully chewed over the burning issues of how United would cope without David Beckham and why it never stopped raining in Oldham.

He was City, I was United, so we had plenty to rib each other about. I was always careful to meet my pals when Dad was out, and only when all my chores were finished in the house. I knew instinctively Dad would not approve of me having fun, especially not with boys. Dad was known on the street as Nicotine Nose Nigel because of his yellow nose hairs stained with years of heavy smoking. His fingers were yellow too. It was curious for me to hear the nickname, because I did not see my father as a figure of fun or ridicule.

To me, he was a bogeyman; someone to be feared at all times.

That summer, Dad's parents invited me to stay with them for a couple of weeks, and I was over the moon when Dad agreed and Grandad arrived to collect me. They had a large and beautiful home in Manchester, and I was given my own bedroom complete with a TV and video recorder. It felt like five-star luxury. Grandma threw her hands in the air when she saw the state of my clothes and again, she took me on a shopping spree around *JD Sports*. This was the first time I'd been shopping since the Florida trip. When we got home, Grandad taught me how to play golf in the garden and, when I smashed a ball right through a greenhouse window, he simply pulled a comic face and yelled, "Quick! Let's run inside!"

The following week, they enrolled me at Bobby Charlton's Soccer School, a football camp which lasted six hours a day. I was, quite literally, in football heaven. I felt as though I belonged there, as though Bobby Charlton and I could have been soulmates in another life. Every day, I woke with a smile on my face. I slept with my football kit by the side of my bed and my shin pads on my pillow.

When the football camp finished, and it was time for me to return to Dad's, I was bereft. For weeks afterwards, I grieved for the Bobby Charlton Soccer School so much that it felt like a physical loss.

"Stop moping around and get this place cleaned and vacuumed," Dad barked. "You'll feel the back of my hand if it's not done by the time I get home."

Again, I wondered how on earth my grandparents could have produced a son like him.

* * * *

September rolled around and I returned to school, though my attendance was sporadic and my behaviour in and out of class was appalling. I was constantly angry, without understanding why. I got into arguments with the teachers and fights with other pupils. My fury pulsated inside me, like a living being, like an alien clawing its way out through my skin.

One afternoon, out of school time, I got into a row with another girl with the sole intention of hitting her as hard as I could. When I left her, with a bloody nose and a black eye, I expected to feel victorious. Satisfied, smug, at the very least. Instead, I felt deeply ashamed. I was turning into my father, taking my temper out on innocent bystanders. I was becoming a bully. I could not bear that I had inflicted my own pain on someone else and I later found out where the girl lived and apologised to her. From then, I turned my anger inwards – on myself. My knuckles bore the brunt of it, as I scraped them down walls or ran a razor across my skin. Self-harming was, for me, an act of self-hate. It was deeply cathartic to see a row of bloody knuckles because it was a reflection of how little I valued myself.

Early in October, I came down with toothache which got worse as the days went on. Dad knew I was ill but showed little interest. One afternoon, because he was out, I went to see Katrina and Sammy who lived a few doors down. Their Mum, Belinda, was lovely and had taken me under her wing since I moved onto the street. She gave me painkillers and clove oil and then said, "Would you like to stay here tonight? You can sleep in Katrina's room. I'll speak to your dad about it, no problem."

Without me having to explain, she seemed to understand that Dad was difficult. The next morning, still in agony, I stayed in bed whilst Katrina and Sammy went off to school.

"Don't worry, love, your dad knows you're here and he said it's fine," Belinda told me. "Here, take these painkillers."

By mid-afternoon though, I was becoming edgy. I worried Dad might not be quite as understanding as Belinda thought. With my face throbbing, I made my way home. I was no sooner through the front door than Dad rounded on me, pinning me up against the wall.

"Give me a good reason why I shouldn't hit you," he shouted.

"I don't kn – " I began.

Before I could finish my sentence, I felt a crack on the side of my head which chimed with my toothache and seemed to reverberate right around my skull. Still, I had got through it without crying, and I thought that was it. Punishment complete. I staggered over to the sofa, to get my bearings a little. But in the next minute, Dad flung a heavy ashtray, made from green glass, which hit my knee with a dull thud. The pain was excruciating, and I thought he'd smashed my knee-cap.

"What do you think you're doing, sitting down?" he

hollered. "You've been out all night. You've got work to do. Get the washing on."

Trailing my injured leg, I hurried out of the living room and went upstairs to collect the laundry. When I came back down, he snapped, "You've missed some. Go and get the rest of it."

Practically dragging me upstairs, into my bedroom, he threw back the duvet to reveal my pyjamas. They weren't laundry, they didn't need to be washed. But I didn't dare contradict him.

"Sorry," I stuttered, scooping them into my arms.

Dad seemed deranged, lunging at me in the bedroom and chasing me downstairs. In the hallway, he threw me against the wall and began pummelling me in the ribs. I had never been hit with such force before and it felt as though my heart and lungs would rupture with the pain. In the next moment, I heard a knock at the front door, and I screamed for help. I had nothing to lose, I thought he was going to kill me. Katrina came rushing into the house; she was calling on her way home from school to see how my toothache was.

"It's nothing that she doesn't deserve," Dad said to Katrina.

Then, he rounded on me with a look of pure disgust and snapped, "I'm going out now. When I get back, I will hit you with everything which hasn't been cleaned away."

As the front door slammed, I slid down the wall and into a crumpled heap on the floor.

"Please, ring my Mum. Get some help," I gasped.

I hadn't spoken to Mum for nearly 10 months since leaving her house. But I had nowhere else to turn. Katrina made the call and thankfully the urgency in her voice convinced Karl and Mum to come and collect me there and then. I was in too much pain to pack my belongings and I was anxious to escape before Dad returned. I was wearing my school uniform from the day before, and I managed to grab my army cadet uniform, and my box of certificates and trophies. The rest, I left behind and later learned that Dad had set a fire in his back garden and burned the lot.

In hospital, it was confirmed I had three broken ribs. Still in shock, I told the staff that my father was responsible for the attack, and the police came. But by the time an interview was scheduled, a few days on, I had lost my nerve. I was frightened of Dad and how he might react. And I had a warped sense of loyalty, too, it didn't seem right to turn on him in that way. What would my grandparents think? He was, after all, my father. I withdrew my complaint, saying I had made a mistake, and nobody pushed me any further on it.

Perhaps at that point, I could have been saved. If a police officer or a social worker had looked further into what had happened, my life might have been very different. I was teetering on a precipice waiting for someone to either pull me back or push me over.

14

BACK AT Mum's, I had to return to school full-time, with the teachers demanding to know where I had been and why I had been absent for so long. I had to wear my horrible old coat and my tight shoes. Worse still, I couldn't play football, because of my broken ribs. I couldn't even breathe without pain and when I smiled, it was agony. Good job, then, that I had very little to smile about. Worst of all, I knew I was not wanted at my mother's house. I was like a stray animal, chancing my luck at one address after another, never welcome anywhere.

As soon as my ribs began to heal, I went out looking for work. The atmosphere at home was toxic. Mum shuffled past me as though I wasn't there. And Karl and his friends continued to tease and bully me. More than once, Ray and Deano blindfolded me and spun me around the living room, laughing helplessly as I sobbed. When I tripped over, they'd shout: "Oi, golf club legs! Looks like your legs have finally snapped!"

On my first day of job-hunting, I was offered a spot

washing pots at a chicken stall on Oldham market. I was paid £7 for two hours work, three or four times a week. I needed the money, but more importantly, I needed to stay out of the house. My boss was lovely, she seemed to intuit that I was unhappy, and did her best to look after me. I had only two outfits, my school uniform and my cadet uniform, and it took months before I was able to save enough to buy a few T-shirts and a pair of jogging bottoms from the market stalls.

One Saturday morning at work, I was emptying the bins when I heard a voice which curdled my blood.

"Lou-Lou! What are you doing here?"

"It's my job," I muttered, head down, not wanting to cause any fuss. But inside, my stomach swirled with foreboding.

"You think you're smart, reporting your own Dad to the police?" he said, his voice louder now. "Eh? Is that it? You think you're funny?"

I was frightened of him, but I was frightened too of losing my job. Quickly, I whipped off my apron, yelled something to my boss, and ran. Dad chased me all through the market, yelling angrily. When I finally managed to lose him, I ran back to the stall, breathless with apology.

"I really should sack you on the spot," frowned my boss.

"I know, I'm sorry," I said. "It won't happen again."

But really, I had no way of knowing that. Soon after, Dad turned up at army cadets. In truth, I had only continued attending because I wore the outfit most of the time. It was bad enough having to nip to the shop in my cadet uniform, without then admitting that I wasn't even a member of the organisation. On this particular evening, I was inside with all the other kids when I heard Dad bawling at the entrance. Two of the adults ran to investigate and eventually, after a lot of shouting and swearing, he left. But that was my last evening at cadets. I could not bear the sideways glances, the pointed comments, worse still, the sympathetic murmurs.

My 15th birthday passed without any fuss and again, my heart was torn in two, thinking of my foster family and of happier times. A shower of technicolour memories fell like rose petals around me, precious and heartbreaking in equal measure. Squeezing onto the sofa with my older siblings to watch a Saturday night film. Sitting on Dad's knee as he taught me to tie my shoelaces. Holding Mum's hand as we walked, arms swinging, to Irish dancing classes. Even now, I missed them so much. I just wanted my old bed and my home. I was homesick for somewhere that no longer existed and possibly never had.

Suspended in a sort of limbo, I wandered the universe like a little refugee, without a place to call home.

****

When the warmer weather came, I began staying out after work with my friends. We found a place that sold 24 cans of lager for £7, which, for two hours work, seemed like a bargain. It was cheap lager, warm and watery, but I didn't care. I loved the camaraderie out at the park, swigging back drinks in between mass games of football. And I enjoyed the feelings of fuzziness that crept over me after a couple of cans. Drinking didn't solve my problems, but it did kick them a little further down the road, which I was grateful for.

The summer holidays began and, even on the last day of term, I began fretting about a uniform for the following September. My own uniform was too small and worn out. But I knew nobody would buy me a new one. Thinking ahead, I asked my boss to withhold my wages all summer, so that by the end of August, I had a little over £340 owing to me.

"Here," she smiled, handing me a bulging pay packet. "I've popped in a little bit extra too. Now go and buy your uniform before you spend it all."

I went straight to the uniform shop and picked out new shoes, a coat, trousers, shirt and tie. I bought a bag and stationery, too. Trudging home with my shopping bags I expected to feel elated; I had done it. I had saved all that money and I wanted to feel proud. Instead, with each step, the happiness sludged out of me, just as if it was dripping out onto the pavement. What was there to celebrate when, aged 15, I had to buy my own school uniform? How could I possibly feel proud that there was nobody to care about me, nobody to look after me? Everywhere I turned, my life seemed to go rotten. It was as though I was set up to fail. I did not deserve happiness. The joy of my early years, my bedroom with the bunkbeds, my mini football goals in the garden, felt like some sort of passing fantasy; an insubstantial, illusory dream. Gone forever.

One evening, with the rest of my wages, I bought a bottle of paracetamol at the local shop. Sitting on the pavement,

I forced each one down, without a drink. And then, by the side of the dusty road, as litter blew and cars passed, I waited to die. A little further up, on the Tarmac, I spotted a dead squirrel, squashed completely out of shape. My heart went out to the little animal, to his parents and siblings. He would be missed, no doubt, unlike me. A tap on my shoulder jolted me out of my daze and my neighbour said, "Stace, have you taken all these?"

She shook the empty paracetamol bottle in front of me. I shrugged. Like a robot, I allowed her to help me to another neighbour's house, where we found my mother.

"I've taken an overdose," I told her.

She looked at me.

"I don't believe you," she said flatly.

I didn't know what to say to that. I felt she'd had the last laugh, again. Even in death, I couldn't get her attention.

I went home and crawled upstairs to bed. It wasn't until several hours later that I began vomiting violently. I was taken to hospital where the doctors told me I had damaged my liver and the pigments in my skin, and I was lucky that it wasn't worse. But I didn't feel lucky at all. I didn't really feel anything. My overdose was, in hindsight, more of a cry for attention; a plea to be noticed. But at that time, I genuinely felt I no longer wanted to be alive. I could see no future ahead.

One evening, after I'd finished work, my friends made a fire on the edge of the field. Someone had brought butties and crisps and I'd invested my £7 wages in a crate of cheap lager. As it grew dark and chilly, they packed up, one by one, ready to wander off home.

"I'm not going home," I announced.

I hadn't known I was going to say it myself, it was more of a feeling than a decision. I just knew I could not keep putting myself through it.

"That is so cool," said Hayley, my friend. "Sleeping out, under the stars. I'll stay with you."

That first night, we tried sleeping right there, next to the dying embers of the fire. Even without blankets, we figured we might stay warm. But the grass soon grew damp and even breathing into my hoodie to warm myself up, I became cold and shivery. But the cold was not my greatest concern.

"What about snakes?" I said, worriedly scanning the grass in the darkness.

I'd been petrified of snakes ever since I was small. And even though there was only an outside chance of me bumping into a python in Oldham, I was not prepared to risk it. The threat of a snake slithering over me as I slept was enough to keep me wide awake and vigilant all night long.

With the first pink streaks of dawn, Hayley went home to bed. But although my teeth were chattering, and my feet were stone cold, I knew this was preferable to facing Mum, Karl and his mates. The next night, I found a dry, concreted area in front of some flats at the edge of wasteland. It was a kind of car port with a roof but no walls.

"Wow, Stace, you're like Ray Mears," my mates laughed.

But I felt more like a tramp. To them, it was an adventure, a bit of fun. To me, it was real life. I barely slept those first few nights. I was anxious about being attacked − by snakes rather than humans − but the anxiety was real, nonetheless.

And the residents in the flats left early for work, so I had to make sure I was gone before they surfaced. The idea of someone tripping over me, like a bag of rubbish, was mortifying.

As the days passed, I became exhausted. I could barely function at work. I was filthy too, my nails were dirty and my hair needed a wash. The deterioration in my personal hygiene correlated directly with the slide in my quality of life. Ever since leaving the Robinsons my standards had slipped, in every way. At the end of the week, I risked a trip back to the house when I knew they'd be out, so I could have a quick shower and grab some snacks. But I didn't stay long. Sandra, Dad's former partner, lived opposite the flats. And when I bumped into her one morning, she offered to make me breakfast and run me a hot bath.

"Stace, you shouldn't be sleeping rough," she frowned. "You're still a child. Why aren't social services helping?"

"I don't want their help," I interrupted quickly. "They'll just cause me more trouble."

I was worried she might report me herself. Realising I needed a new place to sleep, I came across a disused lock up, damp and mossy, with grass growing up the walls. I had a brief flashback to my bunk bed with my David Beckham book on the shelf and my football posters on the wall. How had it come to this?

The lock-up was dank and creepy; the sort of place I might find a swamp monster, I thought with a shudder. Worse still, a boa constrictor. But at least there was no risk of being discovered by anyone. Here, I was hidden away and completely on my own, a prospect which filled me with both relief and alarm.

As I huddled against the crumbling wall, I heard a scurrying sound nearby. Shivering, I realised I was not alone, after all. But I preferred the rats and the killer snakes to being at home. For three long and lonely weeks, I slept rough. The evenings were not so bad, my friends were around, and we played football and built fires in the park. But after they went home, I felt desolate – like an outcast. Even with a ball at my feet, I no longer felt truly safe. I had stopped playing for a football team, I couldn't afford boots or bus fare or subs, and anyway, the game didn't give me the same joy it once had. I was falling out with football, at the same time as falling out with myself. And the further I drifted from the sport, the further I drifted from myself.

* * * *

Into my fourth week of sleeping out, I lost my job at the chicken shop because I kept on mixing up orders. It was hardly surprising, I'd had not enough sleep and too much lager and it was not a good combination. A couple of days later, I was messing about in the park with my friends, when we spotted two police officers walking towards us.

"Which one of you is Stace?" they asked.

My heart dropped.

"Me," I said quietly. "Sandra told you about me, didn't she? I knew she would."

I had no idea what to do next. Mum didn't want me. Dad

didn't want me. My foster family didn't want me. Perhaps I would have to go into care. But then the officer said, "No, she didn't. But as a matter of fact, she has said she'd be happy for you to stay with her, on a temporary basis. While you sort things out at home."

Briefly, I rolled my eyes at the idea I might ever be able to sort things out at home. But I was delighted by the invite.

"Yes, please," I said. "I'd like that."

Living with Sandra was a short-term plug, and I knew I'd have to find something else soon. My 16th birthday came, and I celebrated with my mates in the park, drinking the same cut-price lager as always. It was supposed to be a landmark birthday, the start of my adult life. But instead, I felt trapped and hopeless. Being 16, I was old enough to apply for copies of my social services records and find answers to the many questions which had buzzed around my head since that day in the park. The social services offices were not far from school, so I called in and filled out the necessary forms.

"I'd like copies of my records please," I said. "I need help. I have nowhere to go, I hate it at home. Could I please have a flat? I'll even go into a children's home if they'll have me?"

"It's not that simple," said the lady on the desk. "You can't just move into a flat or a children's home."

A few weeks later, I got a call to say a social worker would come to Sandra's to discuss my records. I felt a strange mix of dread and relief on the day of her visit. Much as I needed to see what was written, I knew it would be distressing. The social worker arrived and, when I asked for the records, she hesitated.

"It's not that simple, I'm afraid," she said. "We can't let you see your records. I'm sorry about that."

My mouth hung open in objection.

"Are you serious?" I said eventually. "These are my records. These things happened to me. I want to see them."

She sighed.

"There are things in there which we just don't feel you're ready to read," she said. "I'm sorry. But as I explained, it's best to wait a while."

And with that, she was gone. I had so much pressure, building in my chest, I felt like I might burst. How could she not see that not knowing was worse than anything? And telling me there was something unpalatable in there, something I couldn't cope with, just left me with even more questions. My life seemed to be all holes and nothing solid. I needed someone to help me fill in the gaps. But as usual, the social worker had decided what was best for me, without even listening to what I had to say.

Pulsating with fury and frustration, I went out to the side wall of the house and scraped my knuckles until a blob of fresh red blood covered each one. I sagged with relief, but like all artificial highs, it didn't last. By the time I went back inside, my anger was building again. As this was my final year at school, I should have been preparing to sit my GCSEs. But I had failed to submit my art coursework and so was not allowed to take the exam. I'd passed my PE practical with flying colours but had not completed my project, neither had I been to lessons, so was told I had no chance of passing. And even though I was allowed to sit science, I refused to do so. I pretended I didn't want to do well, but deep inside I was scared of failure. Always, running parallel alongside the dysfunctional chaos, was the ghostly image of another Stace, well-balanced, well-fed, well-loved. What kind of girl would I have been if I'd stayed with the Robinsons? Certainly, I'd be sitting a whole string of GCSEs, probably passing most of them. More importantly, I'd want to pass. I'd want to excel – for them, as well as for myself.

Now, I didn't even have anyone to buy my school uniform. There was no one to impress. No one to disappoint. It was like a film reel playing at the back of my mind all the time; a utopian vision of how life might have been. I remembered my foster dad, in front of the TV, watching *Bullseye*.

Here's what you could have won Stace.

But I hadn't won a thing.

15

TWO WEEKS before my GCSEs began, I had a startling change of heart. One of my friends was planning to study health and social care at college and, as she described the course, I had to admit, I fancied it myself. Up to now, I had been so set on failing, so determined to flunk all my exams. But for what? Who exactly was I punishing, aside from myself? Nobody else was the slightest bit interested.

"You can still do it, Stace," she told me. "You only need a D in Maths and English. You've two weeks left."

I wrinkled my nose while I thought about it.

"What about money though?" I asked. "I need a full-time job. I can't afford to go to college."

"You can apply for EMA, it's £30 a week," she replied. "You could carry on working part-time as well. You'll be fine."

I thought of my trophies, under my bed. *One day, I will make something of myself…* It was worth a shot, I decided.

For those two weeks I worked as hard as I could, catching up on work I'd missed, borrowing notes, digging out old textbooks. I sat Maths and English GCSE and hoped for the best. After leaving school, a long summer stretched out before me, a delight for most of my peers but something which held mixed appeal for me. With my exams over, I got a job as a glass collector in a local pub, but I still had to fill my time somehow. On occasion, I had to nip home, to collect a few more clothes or belongings. I hated even walking up the street, and the air prickled with hostility the minute I walked through the door. I imagined the walls whispering about me.

She's back. That skinny girl. That bloody nuisance. When will she ever learn we don't want her here?

Like a stomach bug, I had been passed, most of my life, from one household to the next, each one eager to get rid of me as quickly as possible. I took on extra hours at the pub, I didn't want to get in Sandra's way, and I stayed out as much as possible. I paid her rent from my wages, but I knew this was just a stop-gap solution. One night at work, my phone bleeped with a message. When I saw Mum's name flashing on the screen, I gulped. I hadn't heard from her for months. And when I opened the message, my jaw dropped in aston-ishment.

Hi Stace, will you come and see me?

I had to re-read it to make sure I wasn't mistaken. This was the first time Mum had ever reached out to me. If the message had come from Mars, it could not have been more unexpected. Despite years of experience warning me otherwise, I felt my heart skip as I left work and headed for Mum's house. Maybe, just maybe, this was a new start for us both. When I arrived, it was after 11pm and the house was in darkness. Tentatively, I tapped on the door, and Mum's friend, Lara, answered, the same lady who had gifted me the bags of spare pennies, years earlier.

"Where's Mum?" I asked.

"Oh, she went to bed, love," Lara replied. "You can stay over if you like. Your bed is made up ready."

Perplexed, I did as she said. And the next morning, when Mum came downstairs, she didn't seem especially pleased or surprised to see me. It was as though she'd forgotten I'd ever left in the first place. She didn't mention the text message at all.

"Am I okay to stay here?" I asked tentatively.

"If you like," Mum smiled.

It was weeks before I found out Mum had not sent the text message at all. She'd gone to bed, leaving her phone unlocked downstairs, and Lara had written the message to engineer a reunion between us. Mum knew nothing about it. Deep down, I'd known it was too good to be true, yet it hurt, all the same. Whatever hope and happiness I'd felt just drained away leaving me empty inside. I did not belong here, after all.

* * * *

Collecting my GCSE results, in August 2005, I was pleased to be awarded D in Maths and English, the grades I needed for college. But there was an element of disappointment too. I'd started high school with straight A grades, and here I was with two Ds. Such was the pattern of my life.

The following month I started college, and quickly settled in. My tutor, Diane, was lovely and immediately took me under her wing. She went out of her way to make sure I understood the lessons and the assignments. Occasionally, my old frustrations crept back in, and I would lose patience, banging on the desk. But instead of reacting angrily, Diane was calming and sympathetic. And when she spotted my knuckles, bloodied and bruised, she pulled me aside after class.

"What's going on, Stace?" she asked.

"I'm not wanted at home," I shrugged. "Just the way it is. I've nowhere else to go."

"Well, if I can help, please let me know," she said. "Your college work is excellent so far and I'm really pleased. I think you should be proud of yourself."

Her words were like the sun coming out from behind a cloud. Beaming, I thought of the trophies and certificates under my bed. *I can make something of myself. I can do it.* Years earlier, after the football tournament, I'd given up on ever achieving anything. But Diane's encouragement gave me the motivation I needed to tentatively start believing in myself again. Even when I was late for class, she did not record it, as she knew my EMA payments could be removed as a result. I relied on my EMA to buy toiletries and deodorants and, keen to make a good impression at college, I began showering two or three times a day. I saved my wages for a haircut, too. I saw it all as part of a positive transformation, yet I was going from one extreme to the other, not washing at all to washing too much. I strived for normality, with no idea of what normal actually was. Against the odds, I finished the first year of my course with a distinction.

"Top of the class!" Diane shrieked, waving my results in the air. "I knew you could do it! Congratulations."

I was over the moon, but I knew better than to try to share my good news at home. Instead, I hugged my secret to me, and the warmth filled me with joy and optimism for my future. I could not wait for the second year of college to start in September 2006. Finally, I was going to make something of myself. In October, one month into the new term, my phone rang with a number I didn't recognise.

"Hello Lou-Lou," said a syrupy voice, and a shiver rippled down my spine. "I got your number from Nanna. I want to talk to you."

I was cursing myself for taking the call, wondering how I could get rid of him, when he said, "I want you to know I've changed. I've been to anger management classes. I never lose my temper these days. Honestly, you should see me. I'm like a different man!"

He chuckled a little, and sounded so convincing that a part of me desperately hoped it was true.

"I've got a new partner," he continued. "And she's about to have a baby, so you'll soon have a new brother or sister."

I had always loved babies and I felt myself melting. Ever since little Billy had died, I'd longed to have another sibling.

"Not only that," he said. "I'm looking after your little sister, Maisie, too. Remember I told you about her? Her mum lives in Essex so I've moved down here to spend some time with her."

I vaguely remembered Dad mentioning a half-sister called Maisie but had never met her.

"So," he concluded. "Just ringing to say hello. I'll ring you again soon."

As he hung up, I realised he hadn't asked a single thing about me. But then, I was used to that. At the start of December, he called me again.

"Just letting you know you have a new baby sister," he announced. "She's lovely. We've called her Mia."

I couldn't wait to meet her and Maisie. But Essex was a long way away and I couldn't take time off college, especially when I was working hard and doing well. I had my part-time jobs too. Two weeks on, Dad messaged me.

Come for Christmas! You could come on the coach from Manchester, and I will meet you in London.

I was torn. I longed to meet my little sisters, but I was wary of Dad. I could not simply wipe from my memory the way he had battered me and fractured my ribs. What I really wanted, more than anything, was to spend Christmas with Mum. But most importantly, for her to want that too. That night, after college, I said to her, "Dad has invited me to Essex for Christmas."

Silence.

"Unless…"

I trailed off. She didn't seem to be listening, so I ran upstairs, got out a big pink bag which I had bought myself, and dragged it down into the living room. Melodramatically, I began packing my things right there in front of her, desperate to provoke a reaction. Throwing in underwear and jeans alongside my precious trophies and certificates, I waited, desperately, for that one word: "Stay." But it did not come. Packing my toiletries, I remembered the Florida Christmas, aged 13.

When you're grown up, I will have nobody. And so I have to choose him.

Those words scissored through me even now, yet still I was prepared to give her another chance. Just one word. That was all I needed. I didn't care about presents, or roast potatoes, or Christmas lights. I just wanted Mum to want me here for Christmas. With tears clouding my eyes, I snapped my bag shut. Just one word. Please say it. Please.

A car horn beeped outside, and Mum cleared her throat and said, "That's Karl, best not keep him waiting."

And off she went. She had not even said goodbye.

Wearily, I dragged my case out onto the path. I felt like I was dragging my heart alongside it. I went to stay with my grandparents, who had agreed to drop me at the coach station for my journey. The next day, I bought myself a £12 return coach ticket to London Victoria, leaving at 6.30am on December 22 and returning on January 4, in time for the new term at college. I'd also just got a new job at *McDonald's*, which was due to start in January.

On the morning of my trip, my stomach was in knots. I didn't even want to spend Christmas with Dad. What was I doing? Why was I going to Essex? I was stuck in a miserable pattern of being hurt by the adults who were supposed to care for me, and in trying to hurt them back I had backed myself into a corner each time. I was so desperate to elicit a response, so anxious for them to love me, that in the end, I achieved the opposite of what I wanted. It had started with my bad behaviour as a little girl, with my foster family, to persuade them to keep me. It had continued when I moved to Mum's and I hoped my bad behaviour might make her send me back. In school, I'd kicked back, hoping for attention. And now, aged 17, I still had not learned my lesson. I had tried so hard to upset my mother but had succeeded only in wounding myself.

* * * *

For the whole journey I sat rigid and tense, wishing I could get off the coach and hoping I would never arrive. As we pulled up at London Victoria, I spotted Dad's spiked dark hair, as he hovered in the coach bay. Memories of that last attack flashed across my mind. Images barged through my consciousness; Dad dragging me downstairs, pinning me against the wall, pummelling my ribs. I could smell the stale smoke on his breath, see those long nostril hairs, just as vividly as if it was happening now.

"Hello Lou-Lou!" he called, as I stepped out into a gloomy London day.

I shook my head, as though it was that easy to rid myself of the memories. Again, I was plagued with doubt. Was I doing the right thing? Dad took my pink bag and strode ahead with me scurrying behind. He didn't speak again until we were standing on a crowded train. "Hang onto the bars, Lou-Lou."

When we arrived at Southend, I spotted a young woman, a little older than me, on the platform. She had a baby in a pram and a small girl with fair hair and wide eyes holding onto her hand.

"This is Gina, my girlfriend," Dad announced.

My attention was split between the lovely little girl who was shyly curling her hair around her finger, and Dad's youthful new partner. She looked around the same age as me. Swallowing my shock, I said, "Pleased to meet you all. Especially you, Maisie!"

I offered her my hand and to my delight, she took it. She chattered away as we walked down Southend High Street, telling me she was eight years old, she liked unicorns and colouring, she did not like soup or sums. I felt my unease dissolving as our conversation tripped easily along. She was so cute. And baby Mia, when I peeked into the pram, was gorgeous too. She was only three weeks old. Perhaps, I told myself, I'd made the right decision after all.

Dad's new flat was above a hardware shop just off a main street. As the door opened there was a musty smell of stale smoke. Maisie skipped up the stairs, eager to show me my bedroom.

"In here," she called, disappearing up a second set of stairs. "Big treat! You're sleeping with me!"

The room, an attic conversion, was huge. There were two beds, with a bookcase blocking the space down the middle, and nothing else. As I plonked my pink case onto the bed, Maisie vanished back down the stairs, and I heard Dad come in behind me.

"There are a few rules here," he said as I unpacked my toiletries and arranged them on the bookcase.

"First, you help out around the place."

Remembering his strict approach to household chores, I nodded. This was no surprise.

"Second, you must call Gina 'Mum'."

I gulped. Was this some sort of sick joke? The word Mum had lost all meaning for me. I could not face using it again on yet another new individual. I did not want to call her Mum, just as I did not want to call him Dad. Besides, she looked only a couple of years older than me. It was absurd. But again, I remembered the pain from my broken ribs, and I knew it was unwise to argue.

"Yes, fine," I said.

"Thirdly, give me your coach ticket," he said, holding his palm out flat.

I presumed he wanted it for safe-keeping, and I handed it over immediately and then continued my unpacking. Dad held the ticket in the air, like a prize, before ripping it ceremoniously into small pieces.

"You don't need that," he said, and then he turned and went back downstairs. My mouth hanging open, I stared after him. What on earth was he thinking? But again, I was wary of getting into a row with him. I had only just arrived here after all, and it was nearly Christmas. Besides, with my next EMA payment, I could buy myself another. This wasn't a disaster.

Even so, I was apprehensive as I went downstairs to the living room. What would he do next? Dad was sitting at the dining table, with pages of paperwork spread out in front of him. He turned to me angrily and said, "See all this? These letters are all about you. Come and look, Lou-Lou."

I hung back, eyeing him suspiciously.

"I didn't do that," he said, jabbing a finger at one document. "Or that! And that was not me."

His voice was rising, and he sounded increasingly manic: "In fact, I didn't do any of this. I didn't do a thing. I didn't break your leg. I didn't do those bruises or those bites on your face either."

I had no idea what he was talking about. At his insistence, I sat down next to him, to look through the bundle of papers he had compiled about me over the years.

"Read this," he demanded, thrusting a bundle of paperwork in my face. "All lies! And look, here's a letter I wrote to you when you were small, but I wasn't allowed to give it to you."

None of this made any sense to me at all. I was exhausted. I'd been up since 5am, travelling since 6am, and all I wanted to do was sleep. I couldn't even focus on the documents in front of me. Despite my delight at meeting my two half-sisters, I was already beginning to regret my visit.

16

THE NEXT couple of days passed by relatively peacefully. It was awkward calling Gina 'Mum' and I sensed she felt the same. She was quiet and shy, and I learned she was 21, four years older than me and 17 years younger than Dad. But we both played along with the charade with a tacit acceptance that it was best for everyone. I loved helping out with Maisie and Mia and when they were in bed, Dad rolled cigarettes for me, and we watched wrestling on telly.

"Just like the old days, eh Lou-Lou," he grinned, and I forced a smile in reply.

On the evening of December 23, Dad invited a couple of friends from the pub. I sat quietly and listened as he bragged about being in the army and fighting in the Gulf War.

"I've a drawer full of medals upstairs," he said proudly.

I knew already that this was complete fantasy as he had failed an army medical .

"Look, this is where I was stabbed on active duty," he said as they made appropriate sounds of admiration.

His tall tales continued as he claimed he'd had a top job at the Ritz hotel in London, where he'd earned tens of thousands of pounds.

"Everything I earn is in a secret bank account for Lou-Lou," Dad announced. "My favourite girl."

I squirmed with embarrassment both on his behalf and my own.

Christmas Day came, and I loved celebrating with Maisie. Dad and Gina had bought me a bath bomb and some toiletries. I didn't often receive gifts and I was grateful. But all day, I couldn't help thinking of Mum. Was she thinking of me? I didn't hear from her all through Christmas. But on New Year's Eve, with my thoughts drifting again to Oldham, I called her.

"Dad took my coach ticket," I said. "Could you and Karl please pick me up? I know it's a long way. I'll pay the petrol."

I heard her consult briefly with whoever was in the background and then she said, "No, they said it's too far sorry."

How was I going to get home?

At midnight, I watched from my window as the New Year fireworks exploded with colour in a sodium-lit sky and I had the strangest impression that I was imprisoned here, and I might never get away. As quickly as it came, I shooed the thought away. I was letting my imagination get the better of me, that's all it was. But on January 2, with just a couple of days to go until the start of term, I started to really fret about my coach ticket. By now, my EMA payment would be in my account, a double payment too, because of Christmas. I popped Mia into her pram, wrapped up warm, and called:

"I'm just nipping out, get some fresh air with the baby."

The cash machine was across the street and a little further down. I checked my balance and there was £60, two weeks' payment, as expected. Plenty of money to get me back to Oldham. I withdrew £30 and as I turned, I saw a figure standing in the window of the flat. Dad. Watching my every move.

My skin shrank and prickled with unease, and I had a horrible sense of foreboding. Anxious to act normal, I walked on down the street to the local shop and bought some sweets for Maisie. When I got back to the flat, Dad was waiting, predatorily prowling the living room.

"Is your EMA in?" he asked.

I was startled. I had no idea how he knew about that.

"Yes –" I hesitated.

"Well then, you need to pay your way," he said. "Hand it over."

With my spirit dropping, I gave him the £20 note, along with the change from the sweets.

"That's all I have," I said.

But even as I was panicking, I was already forming another plan. I still had my bank card and £30 in the bank. I would withdraw it later and I would get back to Oldham, somehow. But as though he was reading my mind, Dad nodded towards my pocket.

"I'll have your bank card as well," he said.

With trembling hands, and with the memory of my broken ribs, I did as he said. In that moment, I felt utterly wretched. Another plan shattered. What would I do now? Later in the evening, while Dad was nodding off in front of the TV, I called Mum again.

"Please," I begged. "I really need a lift back. I've no money."

But she couldn't help. I couldn't think of any friends who had cars. I was wary of involving and upsetting my grandparents. I even thought of contacting social services. But I knew how angry Dad would be when he found out. Besides, the authorities hadn't helped me much in the past. I couldn't rely on them. In the end, the day before the start of term, I plucked up courage to speak to Dad. I had no idea why he was keeping me in Essex, but I needed to find out.

"I need to go home, please," I said. "I have to go to college. I have a job, too."

Dad's dark eyes danced with malevolence.

"You don't need to go anywhere," he sneered. "You belong here now."

"But why – " I began.

The words died in my throat as I caught the look of pure fury on his face. It was my cue to be quiet. That night, I messaged a male pal from college, asking if he could think of a way to get me home. He called me back, and though he was sympathetic, he couldn't really help.

"I'll send you my notes from the start of term," he offered. "So you can catch up."

As I ended the call, Dad marched into the bedroom and snatched my phone from my hand. I could only watch, despairingly, as he smashed it against the wall again and again until it was shattered.

"You're not going home," he hissed. "I've told you once, you belong here."

All my life, I had wanted to belong. I had longed for someone to want me. The irony was, I had that now. Dad was so desperate for me to stay, he wouldn't let me leave.

It was all I had ever dreamed of, yet suddenly this flat was the last place on earth I wanted to be.

* * * *

Over the next few days, Dad flipped between moods with alarming fluidity. One night, he cooked me tuna pasta, which he knew was my favourite. Afterwards, he put a film on TV about football hooligans and insisted we watch it together. Everyone else was in bed. He rolled me a cigarette and made me sit right next to him.

"Remember when we used to do this?" he smiled nostalgically. "You had those lovely silky pyjamas."

Uncertainly, I nodded. I didn't like the tone of his voice; it was creepy somehow. I was tired, too, because I'd been up early, helping with the children. With the warmth of the gas fire lulling me to sleep, I felt my eyes closing.

"Stay awake Lou-Lou," Dad snapped, poking me in the ribs. "Watch the film!"

The next time my head lolled forward with sleep, I felt the tip of his cigarette touch my leg. I shot up, yelping in pain, convinced it must have been an accident. But Dad said, "There, that'll keep you awake won't it. Every time you doze off, I'm going to burn you."

Too scared to object, and definitely too scared to fall asleep, I sat and watched the rest of the film in silence. The following day, we watched a Manchester United game on TV. Dad had switched from Manchester United to be a West Ham fan, but he still enjoyed football, and it was something we had in common. I did my best to make conversation, hoping I might be able to talk him into letting me go home.

"Good free kick, Dad, do you think?"

"Yeah, should have been a yellow card for that tackle though."

He was perfectly pleasant, for a short period at least. But after the match ended, and Maisie and Mia were in bed, he pulled the furniture to one side and said, "Right, 100 sit-ups Stace, fast as you can. No cheating."

Inwardly I groaned, but I knew better than to argue. Luckily, I was quite fit, but under Dad's critical eye I soon ran short of breath. I paused, just for a moment, with my head hovering off the floor. In the next second I felt a crack against my ear as Dad's boot made contact. I felt like curling up into a ball and sobbing, my ear was throbbing so badly I worried that my ear drum had actually burst. But it was important not to show any kind of emotion. That would only make him worse. Screwing my eyes shut, I pulled myself up for another sit-up.

"We'll make a solider of you yet, Lou-Lou," said Dad with a smile. "I'm proud of you, you know that."

And just like that, he was back to being friendly again.

I didn't know where I was with him, and each day was like tiptoeing over eggshells. Dad seemed to slide between nice and nasty, two sides of the same twisted coin. The inconsistency in his behaviour made him so hard to predict, so hard to gauge, and it was confusing too. I would have much rather he chose one mood and stuck to it. Back then I did not understand that his mood-flips were all part of a deliberate process, his way of bringing me completely under his control. That night, he handed me the baby monitor.

"I want you to get up with Mia tonight when she cries," he said. "I'm counting on you, Stace."

I was puzzled at first, but later appalled, when I heard Dad and his partner having sex through the monitor. I clamped my hands over my ears and put the pillow over my head, but still Dad's grunting filled the room. Why had he given me the monitor? Was it a mistake? I was fast realising that Dad was not the sort of man to make thoughtless errors. The baby monitor was simply another stage in his sordid plans. Two days on, Dad and his partner had a huge row, and afterwards she and Mia left without me even having a chance to say goodbye. I knew I'd miss my baby sister, but I was glad she had got away. And I saw it as a chance to raise the issue of my own departure.

"Dad, I've already missed the start of my new term, I really need to go home, please."

"No, you don't," he replied, his eyes hard and dark as granite. "You belong here. Besides, you're the woman of the house now. You need to look after Maisie and do the chores."

Maisie's new school term began, and I was pleased when Dad made me responsible for the school run. At least it was a chance to get out of the flat, which felt smaller and smaller as each day passed. Some nights, I lay in bed, snatching at shallow breaths, as though the oxygen around me was running out. The air felt too thick, like I was being smothered. In the early hours, unable to sleep, I'd stand at the bedroom window, looking out across the town and beyond to the capital. I felt like Rapunzel, trapped in a tower. There were no bars on the window, no locks, so why did I feel like a prisoner? Why did I feel that I could not leave?

17

ONE AFTERNOON after school, Maisie needed to go to the library to find a book about ladybirds for her homework. As we walked inside, I spotted a row of computer screens, and I suddenly had an idea.

First, we found a few books for Maisie and then I sat her down next to me at the terminals. Quickly, I tapped out an email to my college tutor, explaining I was delayed in Essex, but promising I would be back soon. I was more concerned about her thinking badly of me than I was about missing my college work. After all the support she'd shown, I didn't want her to think I'd simply moved on. To my surprise, her reply came almost instantly.

Try to get back as soon as you can, she wrote. *Is everything okay? I was a bit worried when you didn't show up first day back.*

With a cathartic rush, I typed my reply, explaining I was stuck in Essex with my father with no return ticket, no money and no phone.

I've no way of getting home, I wrote. *And even if I did, I'm scared of what Dad would do. He's very violent. He doesn't want me to leave.*

My heart thudded against my ribcage as I read my email. And then, as my finger hovered over the send icon, I deleted the lot. I just couldn't do it.

All the way home, as Maisie chatted away, I wracked my brains. Mum wouldn't help me. I couldn't confide in my friends or in my tutor, I thought that would make the situation worse, and also, I was ashamed. I didn't want people to know what kind of father I had. His darkness cast a shadow over me, too. I thought about going to the police, but wasn't sure a crime had been committed. What would I tell them? Dad would be sure to talk his way out of it, and I would end up with another battering from him. I remembered confiding in the authorities after I was beaten with the belt. Nobody had believed me then. And nobody would believe me now. I would have to wait it out, I decided, and hope that something would soon change.

In the flat, I did all the housework. The cleaning, washing and ironing. Dad was especially particular about keeping the kitchen worksurfaces clean, and he would inspect the black breakfast bar and the wooden dining table forensically, hoping, it seemed to me, to find fault. It was as if he was desperate to find an excuse to punch me. I looked after Maisie, too.

At weekends, I was allowed to take her to play on a car park opposite. I taught her how to dribble with a ball and how to do keepy-ups. I loved spending time with her. She had been a bit quiet and withdrawn when I first arrived, but now we were getting to know each other and she was really coming out of her shell.

"I'm the best footballer here!" she announced, after dribbling past me and scoring in our makeshift goal. But even as we laughed and celebrated, I was always aware of Dad standing in the window, monitoring our every move.

When he was in a good mood, he'd give me a couple of pounds and I was permitted to go to the shop at the end of the street, again, under his watchful gaze.

One day, he sent me to the shop to buy his cigarettes and before I left, I put on a dress and some mascara. I felt I was slowly rotting in the flat, decaying behind the nicotine-stained walls. Putting on some nice clothes and make-up was my way of showing I was still alive. But when Dad spotted me, he slammed his fist onto the table in anger.

"Get back up those stairs, wash your face and put your joggers on," he thundered. "You dirty little slut."

Bewildered, I did exactly as he said. My jaw was still swollen from his last punch, and I was not about to risk another. When I got back from the shop, Dad made me stand against the wall and he pushed a credit card into my mouth. Then he feinted a punch at my face, making me quiver with fear.

"If I hit you now, both sides of your mouth will be cut to shreds," he chuckled, as though the thought amused him. "It's called a Chelsea Grin."

I had to stand very still, careful to show no fear at all, until he removed his credit card. With his face just an inch from mine, he hissed, "You dress up like a slut again and I will cut your face to shreds."

Three weeks after the start of term, I took Maisie to the

library to return her books, and quickly checked my emails. To my dismay, I learned I'd been kicked off my college course because of poor attendance, and as a result, my EMA payments had been stopped. Feeling absolutely desperate, I laid my head on the desk. What now? And, aside from my disappointment at leaving a course I loved, my main concern was for my tutor. What would she think of me? Would she be angry? My self-esteem was so low it barely registered that my education lay in tatters.

My legs were heavy as we walked back to the flat. I thought of the sand mountain, and once again I felt like I was sinking into sludge. How would I ever get home again? The irony of trying to get back to a place where I was not even welcome was not lost on me. I wasn't sure I even had a home. There was no solidity in the places around me and even less in the people. I couldn't rely on anywhere or anyone.

All I knew was that I was not safe here.

18

WHEN DAD found out I'd lost my place at college, he was unconcerned.

"Best thing for you, Lou-Lou," he said breezily. "Tell you what, I'll see if I can find a college for you around here, okay?"

Numbly, I nodded. It wasn't what I wanted, but it was pointless to say anything. He made an appointment at South Essex College, and I took along my college certificates, which I'd brought from home.

"You've a lot of catching up to do," said the tutor doubtfully. "If you can complete 17 assignments in the next two weeks you can have a place on the course."

Despite myself, I felt a little lift inside. Returning to college would mean Dad would have to let me out of the house on my own. I'd have access to the internet and to an email account. Perhaps this could be my route back home? It was worth a shot. That weekend, I planned to work solidly on my assignments. But Dad said, "I've got tickets for Southend FC, Lou-Lou. Get ready, we're going out."

Ordinarily, I'd have been thrilled to watch a live football

game. But I just wanted to get back to my studies. The following day, he set me to work spring-cleaning the flat. It was late in the evening by the time I started my assignments and I worked almost until morning. In between all my chores and looking after Maisie, I was making good progress.

"How many assignments do you have left?" Dad asked, as my deadline approached.

"I've done 13," I told him. "I have four left, all psychology. They're the hardest ones but I'm going to make a start tonight."

"Oh, I can help you there," Dad announced, and insisted we went straight to the library where he picked out three or four Sigmund Freud books. On the walk home, he pontificated about Freud as though he was an expert.

"You need any help, you let me know," he said, dropping the books into my arms when we got back.

That evening, I'd just put a dark wash on when Dad appeared at the kitchen door holding a white T-shirt.

"I'm going out and I need this washed," he said.

I nodded apologetically towards the washing machine.

"Sorry," I said. "As soon as this cycle is done, I'll do whites."

I felt a whoosh of anger hurtling towards me a second before it erupted in my face.

"You will wash it now!" he bawled, throwing the T-shirt to the floor. His lips were foamy with spittle, his face wobbling with rage. He swept my legs from under me, and I fell into a clumsy heap on the kitchen tiles.

"Do you want to get up?" he yelled. "Do you?"

"Yes, please," I whimpered. "Yes."

As I put my hands out, ready to stand up, he kicked me back down again and laughed.

"Do you want to get up?" he asked again.

We went through the same sick cycle, over and over. Every time, he let me get a little closer to standing up, before kicking me back down again.

"Oh, Lou-Lou, you just don't learn," he sighed, as though I was a failed project. "Now get this T-shirt washed before I ram it down your throat."

After he had gone, I could barely move. One side of my body was mottled with angry, purple bruises and my face was red and swollen through a mix of pain and tears. Somehow, I managed to take Maisie to school the next morning. I didn't want her to know what had happened. But I was too ill to complete my college assignments, which, I realised, was precisely what Dad had planned all along.

"You missed the deadline," he remarked sarcastically. "What a shame."

In tears, I went to my room, but Dad followed and from the doorway he threw a packet of painkillers at me.

"Go on, kill yourself if you're so unhappy," he jeered. "Do it! Take the lot! See if I care!"

He banged the door shut and I stared at the packet of tablets. They felt like the only way out. But then I thought of Maisie. I couldn't just abandon her, no matter how tempting it was.

With my education in ruins, I was stuck in the flat, day after day, the stagnant smell of cigarette smoke and cheap aftershave calcifying in my lungs. Aside from the school runs,

I rarely had a chance to go outside. Dad thrived on watching me work. I had to iron his shirts until they were perfect. I had to scrub the kitchen until it shone. Everything had to be done to a military standard. One day, Dad sent me out to buy potatoes from a shop across the road.

"Get one of those brown sacks they have outside on the pavement," he told me. "Better value to buy bulk."

I could feel dad's eyes boring through the back of my head as I crossed the street. When I walked into the shop, the owner raised his eyebrows.

"These sacks are heavy," he said. "25kg. Sure you can manage?"

I was afraid of going back without it, so I had to give it a try. But he was right, even with his help lifting it onto my shoulders, I staggered under the weight. Looking up, I spotted Dad following my every move. At the crossing, I put my hand out to steady myself on a lamppost and I dropped the potatoes. The sack was too heavy for me to pick up on my own. Eventually, Dad walked downstairs and came outside.

"Lou-Lou, you're such a weakling," he scoffed, tossing the sack over his shoulder. "See how I picked that up? No problem."

Like the sit-ups, and the Chelsea grin, much of Dad's focus was on physical prowess. He was abnormally obsessed with showing off his own strength, even against his own 17-year-old daughter. He raced ahead, whenever we were out walking, anxious to prove he was faster and fitter than anyone else. He wore tight T-shirts and skinny jeans to showcase what he felt was a body to be proud of. Another time, he said to me, "I used to hit you in the stomach when you were a baby until your pram was rocking back and forth. You were the only baby in the country with a six pack!"

He laughed manically. To him, it was proof he was a real man. To me, it was proof he was a monster. Despite his fascination with physical toughness, Dad was content to watch me doing all the chores every day while he spent his time sitting at his computer.

One evening, Dad went to the pub leaving me to babysit. When he returned he had a woman with him, only a few years older than me.

"Lou-Lou," he called. "Come downstairs, I need you to meet my friend."

"Hello," I said hesitantly.

She looked a little awkward too. Dad pulled her closer to him and kissed her full on the lips for a few minutes. I squirmed and looked away, feeling more and more uncomfortable.

"Your turn now, Lou-Lou," Dad said.

I stared at him in confusion.

"You kiss her," he clarified.

"I can't," I began, but as his eyes darkened, I hurriedly changed my mind. I reached up and kissed the woman briefly on the cheek. But that only seemed to infuriate Dad even more.

"No!" he snapped. "Put your tongues in! Proper kissing!"

I recoiled in horror. I could not believe this was happening.

"You're my dad," I said quietly. "Please don't make me."

Dad grabbed my arm and steered me firmly into the kitchen.

"Do as you're told!" he spat. "In about 10 minutes, come into my bedroom. Wait there until I tell you to leave."

He finished off with a little slap on my face, a timely reminder to stay in line. With every bone in my body protesting, I opened his bedroom door as instructed to find him writhing and grunting on the bed with the woman. Gagging, I tried to swallow down my vomit.

Liverpool 3, Bolton 0.

The bed wobbled as I perched on the end, and though I closed my eyes, the sounds and smells conjured up a lurid image in my mind.

Newcastle and Manchester United, 2-2 draw.

When the sounds stopped, I tentatively opened one eye and snapped it shut again when I saw my father's white backside just inches away. The woman underneath him looked jaundiced in the half-light, her head lolling drunkenly to the side.

Palace 3, Norwich 1.

When it was all over, I was finally allowed to leave. Back in my bedroom, my mind spinning, my heart thumping, I struggled to keep a grip on my own sanity. I got my certificates and trophies out of my suitcase and held them close to me as though they could somehow help to rid me of my pain.

One day, you will make something of yourself. One day, your life will get better. Keep believing, Stace. Keep believing.

* * * *

Though the woman had vanished by the next day, Dad's disturbing behaviour continued. While Maisie was at school, he called me over to the computer and told me to read a message he'd written. When I crouched down to check the screen, my blood ran cold.

Lou-Lou, I think you're sexy, said the message.

"Go on," Dad said. "Send a reply. I'm waiting."

It felt so surreal. My mouth ran dry as I typed: *It is wrong. You are my Dad. Please stop it.*

Dad read it, shrugged, and pushed me aside so he could type out another message:

Come on. Nobody needs to know. Give me a kiss.

I was appalled. I just had not seen this coming, or perhaps I had not wanted to see it. Was this about control, or depraved lust, or a grotesque blend of the two? Maybe in his mind, sex and control were both the same thing.

I can't, I typed, with trembling fingers. *You're my Dad. Besides, I don't even like men. I'm attracted to women.*

I surprised myself with that last admission. I had never told anyone out loud about my sexuality, and only as I typed, did I realise it was true. I understood my sexual preferences were academic to the argument, but I hoped it might put Dad off in some way and he might leave me alone. But he read my last reply and swatted it aside with his hand.

"Lou-Lou, you're being awkward," he said, speaking directly to me. "I've wanted you for so long. I used to look at you in your silk pyjamas and I fancied you so much. That's why I broke your ribs, you realise that, don't you? I was frustrated because I was so in love with you."

Reeling, I tasted bile rising in my throat and desperately tried to choke it back. I clung to the computer chair as though I was on a dangerous fairground ride and might at any moment be flung off into the air.

"Come on," he coaxed, as if I was being unreasonable. "How about a kiss?"

My gaze flicked to the front door. It wasn't locked. Could I make it there before him? Probably not. Could I make it down the street? Definitely not. As he was fond of reminding me, he was bigger, stronger and faster. And when he caught me, I was in no doubt that he would make me suffer. Besides, even if I escaped, where would I go? I didn't have a penny. I didn't have a phone. He had even changed my email password and taken control of my account. And I couldn't just leave Maisie on her own. I would never forgive myself.

"I won't kiss you," I said, more bravely than I felt. "You're my Dad. It's wrong."

"I'm not really, though, am I?" Dad wheedled. "I didn't bring you up. I'm not your actual Dad. It's only a biological thing."

I felt as if I had gone mad and stepped into a dystopian universe where such statements were seen as acceptable.

"No!" I said again, and I ran to my bedroom. As I lay on the bed, sobbing, Dad appeared at my door.

"You know, I could kill you," he said calmly. "I'd get away with it. I'd just tell everyone you'd gone back to Oldham. I could say you vanished on the journey. And who's going to miss you anyway? I'll tell you, shall I? Nobody, Lou-Lou. Nobody would care one way or the other if you died."

He laughed softly to himself and closed my door. The worst of it was, he was right. Nobody would care one way or the other.

That evening, Dad cooked a chicken curry. My tastes were slowly evolving as I grew older, and I loved chicken curry. He chose the mild paste I liked, he set the table himself and lit a candle. With a sickening lurch of my stomach, I realised this was a romantic dinner and he was trying to seduce me.

"I'm not very well, I can't eat a thing," I stuttered. "I'm sorry."

"You will do exactly as I tell you," Dad replied, spooning rice onto my plate. "Eat it. Or else."

That night, he made me sleep on the floor, next to his bed. I lay on the gritty carpet, rigid and tense, too scared to close my eyes. He was just inches away; the mere sound of him breathing a warning to me. From the floor, I was looking up at everything, the furniture, the walls, the ceiling. His jeans were flung over the back of a chair, his jacket hooked on the back of the door.

Everything was above me and it seemed to sum up my life perfectly, I was on the very lowest level. I must have fallen asleep eventually, because when I awoke, at dawn, Dad had his fingers in my mouth. I screamed in terror, gagging on the stench of his nicotine-stained fingertips, petrified at what he might do next. Or might already have done.

"Go back to sleep, Lou-Lou," he murmured. "There's a good girl. Just sleep."

What I wanted, more than anything, was to fall asleep and never wake up. The following morning, I was standing in the doorway, still wearing my coat from the school run, when Dad came into the living room.

"Look what I've made," he said, holding out a cassette tape. "I've done a mix tape for you. For us."

Inwardly, I balked. Outwardly, I did not react. Dad insisted on taking me out for a drive so we could listen to the new tape. His Ford Escort, parked right outside, had a parking ticket tucked under the wipers, as usual. Dad was not permitted to park there, and he got a parking fine most days, but he simply tossed it over his shoulder, as though he was above such nonsense.

On his new tape was *Teddy Bear* by Red Sovine, *Blanket On The Ground* by Billie Jo Spears, Lisa Stansfield, *All Around the World* and Elvis' *In The Ghetto*. Dad sang along, tapping his yellowy fingers on the steering wheel, as though this was a perfectly pleasant day out. When we arrived at a patch of deserted woodland, he pulled over, killed the engine, and put his hand on my leg.

"Lou-Lou, you know how much I want you," he said. "I always have."

He leaned in to try to kiss me, so I set my mouth in a hard line, clamped shut. No entry. But my father, as he loved to boast, was stronger than me and he easily forced his way through with his tongue. His breath was foul, but worse than that were the yellow nose hairs, so long I felt them scratch against my face. *Nicotine Nose Nigel*. The nickname could no longer make me smile.

"It's wrong," I tried again. "You're my Dad. Please stop."

"I'm not," he insisted. "I don't see it like that. Nobody needs to know. Come on."

He licked his fingers and shoved them down my joggers. I was wearing my favourite white NYC jogging bottoms and I tried to squeeze my legs together quickly to stop him touching me. In a flash, his mood changed.

"Play nice, Lou-Lou," he warned. "Or I will lose my temper. You won't like that."

I was cornered. If I did not submit to the sexual abuse, he would abuse me physically instead. And really, I had no say in either. I was not big or strong enough to hold him off. And even if I was, my spirit was too weak and fragile to fight. I felt hopeless and beaten.

That night, Dad's behaviour switched back to perfectly normal. He cooked pasta while I put Maisie to bed. Then he stretched out on the sofa to watch wrestling on the TV. I could almost have doubted whether the attack had actually happened at all, if not for the stinging between my legs. That night, he made me sleep next to him in his bed, but he did not touch me. The anticipation was just as bad as any attack, my nerves were shredded all night as I prepared myself for him making a move.

There was a cruel irony in all those years of confusion over who my real Dad was. Now that I had found him, he was an ogre. A true bogeyman.

19

OVER THE coming weeks, life settled into a routine which was simultaneously ordered and anarchic; mundane and depraved.

Alongside the domesticity of washing the dishes, cleaning the oven and changing the beds, I was subjected to acts of appalling wickedness and degradation. There was a metronomic misery to my days which dragged me lower than I could ever have thought possible. After the morning school run, Dad usually insisted on taking me for a drive. We listened to those same songs, on a loop, until I grew to loathe them. Just the sound of the opening bars of *In The Ghetto* made me want to scream in protest. When we slowed down, or the car stopped, he took every chance to grope me. One day, he attacked me as The Weather Girls sang *It's Raining Men* on his mix tape. I began to loathe the tape almost as much as I loathed my father. In my mind, it took on human characteristics, and I hated it for playing along, unconcerned, while I suffered. I felt the mix tape, and all the songs, were complicit in my suffering.

"Come on, Lou-Lou," Dad hissed, forcing his fingers into my underwear. "You want me to be nice, don't you?"

The truth was, it made little difference to me whether he was nice or nasty. His version of nice, which made my skin crawl like a million ants were on me, was only ever a precursor to another attack. His good moods signalled simply that he would be expecting something from me in return. It felt like a slow suffocation, he was squeezing my neck, tighter and tighter each day. One weekend, he took Maisie and me to Southend FC again and inquired about me joining a team.

"My daughter's a brilliant footballer," he said. "The best you'll see."

At that time, there was no girls' team, and I was too old to join in with the boys. But hearing him speak about me in such glowing terms left me clouded with confusion and self-doubt. How could he be so supportive, and then so vile, all in one day? Perhaps it was my fault he behaved the way he did. Why was I so easy to hate?

Most nights, I was expected to sleep in his bed, next to him, but he did not touch me. I rarely slept for more than two or three hours, and I longed for a night in a bed of my own. I was mentally and physically drained. One evening when Dad was snoring, I crept upstairs to my bed in the attic and soon fell into a deep sleep. At 5am, I was woken with a bang as he upended the whole bed, sending me flying onto the floor. I hit my shoulder hard as I fell and, from under the mattress, I heard him say, "Time to get up, Lou-Lou. And always remember, I am one step ahead of you. Don't ever try to beat me."

One lunchtime, after our usual drive, Dad told me to get dressed up.

"Nice short skirt, plenty of make-up," he instructed. "I'm taking you to the pub. Going to show you off."

I had just one miniskirt, denim with a graffiti pattern. I'd bought it from a stall on Oldham market when I worked at the chicken shop. When I got downstairs, Dad whistled but then snapped, "No coat. Nobody will see you under your coat."

At the bar, I hung back, immobilised with shame.

"And a Blue Wicked for my girlfriend," I heard dad say, as the landlady poured his pint.

We played pool for a while whilst Dad waited for some friends to arrive. They never materialised, and looking back, I imagine they probably didn't exist. On our way home, unable to suppress my revulsion, I protested, "Why did you say I was your girlfriend? I'm your daughter."

Dad laughed.

"I said it so you could be served with alcohol, so she thought you were older. Stop sulking Lou-Lou."

The way he pronounced my nickname, sugary and gloopy and imbued with tenderness, was repugnant. At home, he was perfectly normal again. Back to being Dad. I couldn't keep up with the changes of character, or with the different roles I was expected to play. I was a plaything, a doll, and nothing more. I didn't even feel human. That night, Dad cooked again, a lovely pasta dish, which he knew I would like. He insisted I stay up late to watch wrestling with him. I no longer enjoyed the sport, it was synonymous with him now. But I tried to show a real interest, naming my favourite as Rey Mysterio and hoping that by co-operating, by playing his game, he might go easy on me. He might, in return, leave me alone. But I was aware my compliance could work against me too. I was falling deeper and deeper into the abyss of the wifely role he had created for me.

As we sat on the sofa, and the TV blared, the space between us prickled with deadly tension. And then Dad leaned over, his lips wet on my ear, and whispered, "I really love you, Lou-Lou. Don't ever leave me."

Repulsed, I ran to vomit in the bathroom. It was yet another harsh irony of my situation that while I had finally managed to stop vomiting after eating, I was now vomiting for another reason entirely.

* * * *

In addition to controlling me physically, Dad also had complete authority over my finances. Since the day he had confiscated my debit card, I'd had no money of my own. I was the puppet, and he pulled the strings, and I had to rely on him for everything. He rolled a cigarette for me when, and only when, he felt I deserved one. It was demeaning to have to ask him for necessities such as deodorant and tampons, and even then, I was not allowed to go out to buy my own. He chose what he felt was suitable and I was expected to be grateful.

Sometimes, I tried to fake my period, to keep Dad away from me. But I had to be careful not to be too obvious, because I would be severely punished if he found out. His punishments were variations on the same sickening theme. Sometimes, I was made to do 100 sit-ups while he stood over me and bellowed. If I failed a single one, he punched me. Or perhaps he would flick his lit cigarette against my bare knees. Other times, he would pin me against the wall with one hand around my neck and punch me in the stomach with the other. When he was really annoyed, he would beat me until I was lying in a heap on the floor.

"I'm one step ahead," he would remind me. "I never use all my ammunition at once and that's how I stay ahead of you. Never forget it."

Oddly, another of his boasts was that he had never been to prison.

"After everything I've done, they can't pin a thing on me," he'd say, as though it was an achievement.

One morning, when I got back from the school run, Dad was brimming over with excitement.

"I've got news!" he said. "We're going to start our own juicing business. You and me, Lou-Lou. What do you think of that?"

I was not expected to answer, Dad was not interested in anyone else's opinion aside from his own. Even so, he must have noticed my reluctance.

"It's a brilliant opportunity. Juicing is the in-thing," he added.

And then his eyes narrowed as he said, "Don't ever leave me Lou-Lou. I need you."

To go with our new jobs as business moguls, Dad decided

we needed new clothes, and that same morning, he drove me to Debenhams. I was mortified as he booked me in with a personal shopper who proceeded to pull expensive suits from the rails.

"We're launching our own juicing business," Dad told her. "So my partner really needs to look the part. A nice suit, sexy but smart. I'm sure you know just the thing."

The shop assistant gave a professional nod and ushered me into a very large changing area with plush seating outside.

"Try these on," she smiled. "See what you think."

She looked me right in the eye, and in that moment, I tried to convey everything in a single glance: shame, madness, terror, confusion, pain. But she of course just bustled past me to unhook the first suit from the hanger. Dad's voice floated over the curtain, and I cringed.

"Let's have a look at you, Lou-Lou. I can't wait!"

All afternoon, I was paraded up and down the changing area like a slave. I might as well have had a chain around my ankle, or a price tattooed on my forehead. Dad sat back and passed comment on every single outfit: "Too loose, too long, too tight, too short. Not that colour. Come on Lou-Lou, give us a twirl. Woah!"

I was thankful when at last it was time to collect Maisie from school.

"None of these suits are quite right," Dad told the assistant, who was probably livid at the waste of her time. "We'll maybe come back another day."

As I changed back into my own clothes, I felt utterly wretched. Dad might as well have chewed me up and spat me out onto the deep-pile carpet of the changing room. For months afterwards, I was haunted by those scenes, shuttering through my mind like the clicking of a camera. I remembered the way Dad had leered at me, his eyes running across my body, as I tried one suit after another. The way he had whooped and whistled appreciatively, like we were lovers.

And to this day, those memories thrash around my head like dying fish with no escape. Aged 35, I cannot wear a suit. Even in job interviews, I cannot dress up smartly. I have to hide myself away in baggy clothes like tracksuits. To me, being completely covered up is a comfort, it is quite literally a safety blanket. For the memory of that day is still raw. The threat is still real.

That evening, Dad announced he was making pizza.

"I've bought the dough but I'm going to roll it out myself," he said. "I know how much you love pizza."

Suddenly, brutally, I was hurtled back in time to my foster home. There I was, aged seven, sitting at the table with Donna and my parents, and a large cheesy pizza in front of us.

How about a game of football after tea? I'll go up front.

I remembered the clean, cottony smell of the house, so at odds with the stagnancy of Dad's flat. How could my life have fallen apart so drastically? Reminiscing over such innocence, such happiness, just made me all the more distressed. The memory was not something to cherish. It was something I had to discard and delete, for my own sanity. Later, as we watched TV, I spotted Dad's car keys on the table near the door.

"Could I reach them before him? Could I get away before he caught me?"

I toyed with the idea, knowing, deep down, it was impossible. But then, almost as if it was scripted, Dad began to snore. He was soon in a deep sleep, arms flung wide on the sofa, mouth open. His nostril hairs quivered each time he snored, and it turned my stomach. What if I never had to see his face again? This was it! This was my chance!

Grabbing the keys, I let myself out of the flat and unlocked his blue Ford Escort outside. Sitting behind the wheel, with my blood pounding in my ears, I burst into tears. What was I doing? I'd never had a single driving lesson in my life, but somehow I managed to fit the key into the ignition and start the car. Both sides of my brain were yelling instructions all at once.

You need to go Stace! You have to get home. This is your only chance.

You can't drive! What if you hit someone? What if you kill a child? An entire family?

Mixed in with the weighty issues, the smaller ones jostled for position:

You might run out of petrol and you've no money! Where are the windscreen wipers? Can you reach the pedals?

Next – the bare truth:

If you can't drive to Oldham, just drive into a wall. Kill yourself. Anything is better than going back in that flat. Anything at all.

I even had a wall in mind, further down the street. But then, I thought of Maisie, fast asleep in her bed, blissfully unaware of my trauma. I couldn't just walk out and leave her. I couldn't do it.

Switching the engine off, I climbed into the back seat, haemorrhaging tears, sobbing at my own inadequacy and cowardice. When it came to it, I couldn't take the risk. I couldn't even kill myself without dithering over it. It would be a long time before I could look back on this moment and see it actually as a show of strength and resilience.

Quietly, I crept back into the flat, replaced the keys, and made my way upstairs to bed. Dad had thrown my pink suitcase away, saying I would never need it again. But in a plastic bag on the floor were my certificates and trophies and my football. One by one, I took them out and solemnly lined them up on my bed.

This time will pass Stace. You will not die here. Your life has purpose.

20

I WAS due to turn 18 in April 2007, and the day before my birthday, Dad drove me to Lakeside shopping centre to choose a gift. Like a zombie, I picked out a pair of blue Timberland boots and then he said, "Do you fancy a burger? My treat."

As we walked down the mall, past crowds of bustling shoppers, I imagined running into the middle of the throng and screaming at the top of my voice: "My Dad is abusing me! He hits me, he controls me. Please help!"

Or I visualised myself sneaking into a shop, whispering it quietly to a shop assistant. Scribbling it down, maybe, on a napkin at one of the fast-food stalls. The possibilities rushed through my head like speeding traffic.

I am being held prisoner. There are no locks and no bars. But I am not allowed to leave. I am being kept against my will, yet here I am shopping!

It sounded bizarre, even to me. And what exactly did I think would happen? Even if somebody believed me, I could hardly expect a SWAT team to descend on the shopping centre, pinning Dad to the floor under the spotlight of an overhead helicopter. No. The police, if they turned up at all, would take my name, tell me not to worry, and then send me home with Dad. And before they got a chance to investigate, Dad would kill me, just as he had threatened. I remembered the bruises on the back of my legs. I winced as I thought of my broken ribs. Nobody had believed me then. Nobody would believe me now.

"Eat your chicken burger," Dad prompted. "I've got a surprise for you on the way home."

We drove back through Kent, and I was perplexed when Dad parked at a new housing development.

"Come on in, Lou-Lou," he beckoned, pushing open the door to a showhouse. "They're expecting us."

I trailed behind as he announced himself to the sales assistant.

"You see, we're opening a juicing business," he told her. "We need more space so we're looking for a new home. Isn't that right, Lou-Lou?"

Frozen, I stared at them both. As we walked from room to room, Dad played the role of enthusiastic buyer to perfection.

"Love the bathroom. Love it!" he said. "Lou-Lou, do you think our sofa would fit in here against this back wall?

"Oh look! This one would be our bedroom. Good size. We've got an ensuite too."

I wondered, wearily, as he prattled on, whether he was delusional, wicked or both. The absurdity of the situation, the nauseating perversion, was too much for me to take, and while Dad stayed behind to chat to the sales lady, I staggered blindly outside to the car. The ground was level and solid, but I had that sinking feeling, and again, I thought of the sand mountain where it had all begun. On the journey back, as Dad's hateful mix tape played, I held my face in my hands and sobbed.

"What's up with you now?" he asked in mock innocence.

"What have I ever done to you?" I asked. "Why do you treat me like this?"

Dad threw back his head and laughed. The more I cried, the more he enjoyed it. He loved to see me vulnerable and weak, because then he could showcase his strength.

Back at the flat, Maisie was filled with excitement at my approaching birthday.

"I've wrapped your present up," she beamed. "And we've got you a cake. I'm not telling you anything else. It's a secret."

My heart hurt as I tucked her up that night. How I wished I could turn back the clock and be a small girl again. I would have willingly remained seven forever, to be allowed to stay with the Robinsons.

Downstairs, Dad was in high spirits, measuring his furniture to check if it would fit in the show house. He had not worked during the whole time I had known him, so I had no idea how he planned to buy a new place. His juicing business, like his army medals and his battle scars, seemed like yet another far-fetched fantasy.

Seizing my chance while he was in a good mood, I plucked up the courage to say something that had been bothering me since I arrived.

"When is Maisie going home?" I asked. "Shouldn't she be with her mum?"

I hated the idea of losing Maisie. But I also knew it was better for her to leave. Dad's face reset in an instant and he snapped, "That's up to me, not you, not her."

I had overstepped the mark, so I kept out of his way, busy with housework, until late evening when I made a sandwich for supper. I was on the sofa, ready to eat it, when Dad called: "You've left crumbs on the worktop! Get this cleared up now!"

Knowing how much he hated mess, I put my sandwich aside and jumped to my feet. But as I turned, I saw Dad was wedged in the kitchen doorway, blocking it completely.

"I'll clean – " I began.

But something in his eyes sent shards of terror through to my core. I was rooted to the spot. His fury crackled like electricity around him, so intense I could almost see it, a dark red whirlpool of rage. I tried to focus on the task, clearing up the crumbs, and I took a step towards him. But it was like I was trudging through wet concrete. And then, quick as a lizard's tongue, he reached out and snatched me up.

Like a ragdoll, he flung me from a height onto the grey sofa in the living room. My sandwich fell to the floor and the plate smashed, but Dad didn't seem to notice. The warning bells were screaming in my ears now. This was not like him to ignore mess. Not at all. He lunged towards me, pinning me against the sofa, his sheer weight squashing the breath from my lungs. Was this another show of strength? Another chance to pat himself on the back? I hoped so. His face was so near mine that I could see each revolting nose hair, each sweaty facial pore. But as he yanked my jogging bottoms down, I realised in cold horror that this was something different. I opened my eyes and mouth wide to scream, but no sound came out. Then I remembered Maisie, sleeping upstairs, and worried she might wake up if I made any noise. Perhaps I was dreaming, and that was why there was no sound? But then a sharp shooting pain down below made it all very real.

It seemed to last forever, Dad crushing me with his bulk, his authority. When it was over, he stood up and zipped up his jeans.

"I fancy a butty myself," he said, and he walked into the kitchen.

Shell-shocked, I lay on the sofa. Earlier that evening, he'd been measuring it to see if would fit in his crazy new house. Had he known then that he would do this? How long had it been planned?

Midnight came, I turned 18, and still I lay on the sofa. Inside, I was an empty shell, yet I felt the weight of him long after he had gone. Today, I still feel his weight. I will feel it always.

* * * *

A couple of hours before Maisie was due to get up, I crawled upstairs on my hands and knees. She bounded onto my bed just after 6am, carrying a card and a gift, all smiles and giggles.

"Happy Birthday Stace!" she beamed.

I arranged my face into a smile. There could not have been a greater disparity between our two moods. She, filled with excitement and love at one end of the continuum, me, swamped with despair and self-loathing at the other.

"Open your present!" she insisted.

Keep it together, Stace. Keep it together.

I could not focus on the football scores to distract me. I did not even remember what football was any longer. Maisie had bought me a keepsake with a 'Sister' verse on the front. Downstairs, my new Timberlands were waiting, alongside other gifts and a cake. There was even a balloon with 18 on it. This was, without doubt, the most extravagant birthday I'd had since leaving my foster family.

It was also the worst day of my life.

In the middle of all the fuss, smiling psychotically as though nothing had happened, was Nigel Taylor. No longer my father. No longer deserving of the title, as if he ever was.

"Happy Birthday Lou-Lou!" he exclaimed.

Keep it together, Stace. Keep it together.

It was a mantra that I would need for a long time to come.

That night, Nigel invited two blokes over from the pub. He bought me two bottles of Blue Wicked and a crate of lager for himself. He put *Jackass The Movie* on the telly and settled back on the sofa to enjoy himself as though everything was perfectly normal. If his mates thought it was a strange way for me to spend my 18th, they did not say. I sat rigid, like a statue, inwardly incredulous that they could not sense even a modicum of my trauma. As they laughed and joked, I stared at the sofa where Nigel was now sitting, where 24 hours earlier, I had died inside.

* * * *

A few days after the attack, Maisie went home.

"Maisie's mum is picking her up from school today," Nigel told me. "So you don't need to bother."

"When is she coming back?" I asked.

"Never," he replied. "I'm going to drop her stuff off later in the week."

Whilst I was pleased that she was away from Nigel, it broke my heart that we had not even said goodbye.

"Why are you crying?" Nigel snapped. "You wanted her to go. You said so. This gives us more time together."

With a surge of panic, I realised that he could do exactly as he liked now, without the threat of being overheard or discovered. It was just me and him.

Later in the week, I was having a bath when the door slowly opened. My heart plunged right down into the water as Nigel's face appeared. The bathroom did not lock and only then, I realised how perilous that was. Without a word, he undressed, slowly, in front of me. My skin tightened as I pulled my knees up to my chest to try to hide myself. Scrunched up, as small as I could, I pressed my back right against the taps. I kept completely still, telling myself if I didn't move, if I didn't breathe, then nothing bad would happen. But I felt so vulnerable. So unsafe.

He undressed and stepped into the bath, fear and menace

sloshing alongside the soapsuds. Still, he did not speak. For a few moments, he sat and looked at me.

And then, he got out.

As he left the bathroom, I shuddered so violently I thought I might be having a seizure. My hands shook and trembled, my whole body was shaking. What was his plan?

At 18, trapped in the midst of the most horrific trauma, I was bewildered and terrified by his behaviour. Looking back, I understand the incident in the bathroom was all about control. Nigel was reminding me he could do exactly as he liked, how he liked, when he liked. He might as well have been dangling me over a cliff edge by my ankles. At any time, he could let go and I would crash to my death on the rocks – which would have been preferable.

I tried to time my next bath when he was out, but realised, in despair, that I no longer had a single moment to myself. Without the welcome release of the school run, I wasn't allowed to go anywhere on my own. And Nigel rarely left me on my own, either.

On the odd occasion he went out, he wasn't gone for long, and he would lock me in the flat. Three days on, when I could stand it no more, I ran another bath. I was part-way through washing my hair when the door opened, and Nigel came in. As before, he undressed and climbed into the bath, but this time, he said, "Let me see you wash yourself, Lou-Lou."

"No," I stammered, wrapping my arms around my chest. "No. It's wrong."

He leaned towards me, trying to kiss my neck, and I pulled away, bumping my head on the wall tiles.

"No!" I gasped.

To my relief, he stood up.

"There will be another time," he said confidently, and he left.

As fast as I could, I rinsed my hair and got out of the bath. I hardly dried myself, I was so desperate to avoid him coming back. As I pushed my arm into my top, I got my hand stuck because it was still damp. My heart raced alarmingly as I tried to fasten my buttons.

Not fast enough.

I spotted a shadow through the frosted glass in the door. I had managed to finish the buttons, but I was still only half-dressed when he barged back in, and this time there was no leniency. I could smell the rage on him, the stench of his aggression muffling his usual odour of stale smoke. He forced himself on me on the bathroom floor and I heard myself scream out from the bottom of a long, dark tunnel. As the echoes travelled back towards me, I felt myself losing consciousness. I was drifting away from Nigel. Away from everything.

When I came round, he had gone. Curling up on the dark green carpet, wedged against the bathroom door to keep it shut, I lay there for hours. Without Maisie, I had nothing pulling me back. No responsibilities. I could have thrown myself from the window. I could have run out in the street and screamed. Anything was worth a try. Even being hit by a passing car would be preferable to this. But it was too late for that now. I no longer had the strength to save myself. I did not matter enough to warrant an escape attempt. Like an institutionalised patient, I simply accepted my fate without question.

I no longer cared whether I lived or died.

After the attack in the bathroom, Nigel behaved as though nothing at all was wrong. My grandparents had sent £20 into my bank account for my birthday, and he took me to a model shop in Southend so I could spend it. He still had control over my finances, and he used my bank card in the shop for payment. Normally, I loved making models but as I wandered up and down the aisles in the shop, I felt listless and indifferent. There was a constant hum of anxiety running parallel to everything I did.

Eventually, I chose a tiny matchstick van, because Grandad had been a driver before he retired, and I felt he'd approve. But I had no interest in building it. I had no interest in anything at all. Any small snippets of self-worth had been completely obliterated. I was being buried alive, a little deeper each day, and again I thought of the sand mountain where this nightmare had started. The little ironies of life had played a very cruel trick on me. Another morning, Nigel woke me before 6am by tipping me out of bed and landing me with a thud on the floor.

"Rise and shine!" he yelled. "You'd be up by now and out for a run if you were in the army."

I stumbled downstairs and began my chores, but he said, "I'm taking you to the park for a day out. Get ready."

Normally, I'd have welcomed the chance to play football. But that felt like a past life to me now. I had no energy at all. I was painfully thin and covered with bruises. I could barely stand up, let alone run with a ball. And deep down, I didn't want to play football with Nigel, because he would spoil and stain the sport that I loved. But I had no choice.

In the park, I went in goal and Nigel smacked shots at me, laughing as they hit me in the stomach.

"Thought you were supposed to be a decent footballer?" he scoffed. "You're crap, Lou-Lou."

At the end of May, he took me to Southend air show for a day out. He seemed quite amiable on the journey there, but when we arrived, he refused to let me buy an ice-cream, or even a drink. I wasn't allowed to go anywhere on my own and yet he powered ahead, taking big strides, so that I struggled to keep up. It was another show of strength, another reminder he was the boss.

"Look," he pointed, as the air display began.

It was impressive, seeing the small planes flying in their formations. But there was a darkness hanging over me, a blanket of melancholy, and I no longer found joy in even the smallest and simplest things. There were groups of kids playing football on the beach, laughing in the sunshine. Memories emerged from the dusty corners of my mind, and I saw myself, aged seven, playing with my friends outside my foster home. There I was, in my Manchester United shirt, tearing up the wing with the ball at my feet, ready to shoot.

Great goal Stace!

It was as though I was two different people, with two different lives. The chasm between them could not have been greater.

21

SINCE THE attacks in the bathroom, I had been too afraid to bathe or to wash my hair. A couple of times, I'd tried to rinse my hair quickly over the sink, but it wasn't the same. My head itched and I longed to wash it properly.

"Your hair's a mess," Nigel remarked. "Come here, I'll wash it for you."

I had no option but to comply. But as I bowed my head over the kitchen sink, and he clicked the kettle on to boil, I heard the desolate clang of a warning bell in my mind. I closed my eyes as he rubbed shampoo into my scalp.

"Ok," he said. "Now for the rinse."

He had barely finished speaking when I felt the most horrendous burning pain on my scalp. Yanking my head away, splashing boiling droplets on my neck and arms, I screamed at the top of my voice. My head felt like it was on fire. When I opened my eyes, Nigel was standing there with the kettle, still steaming.

"Maybe it was a bit hot," he conceded. "Put your head back under and I'll run the cold tap."

I could feel blisters bubbling up on my skin. I was in so much pain, I couldn't think straight.

"Lower your head," Nigel instructed.

Gritting my teeth, I waited for the balm of the cold water. Instead, I felt another splash from the boiling kettle, and I reared backwards, screeching in agony.

"Oops, must have made a mistake, I used the kettle again," he said with a deranged laugh.

Nigel stood and smirked as I scooped cold water from the tap and threw it over my head. But it was too late. My skin was burned and blistered, and for weeks afterwards I could not bear even to brush my hair. There it was, hidden under my hair, a physical sign of my suffering. And there was I, hidden in plain sight, in my father's flat – unable to leave, unable to live.

In addition to the violence, Nigel continued to abuse me on an almost daily basis. One of his favoured approaches was to ambush me from behind as I washed the dishes and try to grope me or kiss my neck. Sometimes, he was sickeningly friendly and flirtatious. Other times, he was brutal and cruel. I hardly knew which was worse. If I objected, or shrank back from him, his temper would quickly escalate.

"Remember, I could kill you," he told me. "Nobody would know a thing. I'm one step ahead of you, Lou-Lou."

After one attack, he seemed inordinately pleased with me and announced a trip to the pub as some sort of treat. My head and body throbbed as I tried to play pool. Nigel bought me a bottle of Blue Wicked, my ignominious reward for a job well done. Another night, while I slept, he burst into my bedroom dragging in a large mirror with a silver pattern round the edge. When I tried to scramble away, across the bed, he simply upended it so that I fell to the floor and then he forced himself on me in front of the mirror.

"Watch!" he ordered. "Watch us in the mirror!"

Afterwards, unable to rid my mind of the images, I broke down, wailing loudly on my mattress. To my own ears, it was unbearable. This was the sound of someone who could take no more. Someone who was dying inside. Nigel must have been irritated by my cries because he appeared at the door brandishing a fistful of tablets.

"Here, take these!" he yelled. "That will shut you up once and for all."

The tablets fell and scattered around me like sweets. And though I did not want to live, I did not see death as an option, either. In my eyeline, from the floor, was the plastic bag containing my trophies and certificates.

This will pass Stace. And you will make a life for yourself. Hang in there.

****

One evening in early June, Nigel forced me to watch as he masturbated in the living room. He made me sit so close to him that he ejaculated over my clothes, and I gagged at the smell.

"Ha, I could have done it in your mouth," he laughed. "Maybe next time you can swallow it."

Another day, he shoved his head between my legs, over

my tracksuit, and though I kept pushing him away, he was much stronger. There were also countless incidents where he would place my hand on his penis, or he would grope me. After almost six months living there, I was simultaneously accepting and compliant, yet shocked to my soul.

Mid-June, I discovered a swelling in my groin which, by the evening, had got considerably worse, and it was painful, too. I decided I needed to see a doctor and set about making plans. It was most unlike me to make any kind of decision, or to have any interest in my own health and welfare. Looking back, I wonder if subconsciously I knew. If my body had realised that this was the turning point, even if my mind didn't. After all, I hadn't sought medical advice when my head was covered with scalding blisters, nor when Nigel had kicked me all over the kitchen. Why would I insist on it now, for a relatively minor problem? Luckily, he went out the following morning, telling me he was seeing a friend and wouldn't be long.

"I want this house clean when I get back," he said, and I nodded obediently.

I knew he had a spare mobile phone in his bedside drawer, I'd seen it when I was cleaning. To my relief, there was no passcode, and it had some charge in it, too. Normally, I would never have dared to use it. But today, I had to take the risk. I quickly found a number for the GP and dialled. It was one of the many strange kinks in Nigel's behaviour, at home he presided over a regime of physical and mental abuse. Yet also insisted I register with the local GP and the library.

"If you can be here in 20 minutes, we can see you," said the receptionist.

I deleted my search pattern and the call and replaced the phone. Then I did something I hadn't done for six months. I took Nigel's spare key, hidden in the kitchen, and unlocked the door. I replaced the key and walked out of the flat, to the town centre. The doctor examined my groin, along with some basic checks.

"I feel very unwell," I told him. "I'm sick a lot. I'm exhausted. I… "

"Could you be pregnant?" he asked, peering at me.

"No," I replied immediately, almost cutting off his question. "Definitely not."

"Are you sexually active?" he asked.

"No!" I protested.

I felt quite offended by the suggestion. In my mind, I was still a virgin. I'd never had a sexual relationship, and to me the attacks by Nigel were an act of violence, not an act of sex. I did not, or could not, accept that they could be both. The doctor wanted to do a pregnancy test, but I shook my head.

Manchester United were beaten by West Ham, last game of the season.

"Here," he said, handing me the test. "Take this away, and when you've done it, I'd like you to come back and see me."

Spurs beat Man City, can't remember the score.

Walking out of the surgery I felt dazed, as though I had a mild concussion. I passed a Connexions centre on my way back and, almost with a will of their own, my legs took me inside and into the ladies' toilets. When the test was positive, I shook my head in disbelief. How could it be when I'd never even had sex? The blue line stared at me, but I shook my head again in furious denial. There was some mistake here. I walked out of the centre and tossed the test into a bin.

Liverpool and Charlton was a draw, can't remember that score either.

But as I walked, what began as a trickle of realisation soon overwhelmed me. Disbelief, terror and revulsion swept over me like a tidal wave of dirty water. Arriving back at the flat, I had no memory of my journey. I saw Nigel's car outside and prepared myself for an explosion of temper. I had no key and had to knock on the door.

"Where have you been?" he yelled as he let me inside.

I hurried up the stairs to the living room, aware he was thundering along right behind me.

"You do not leave this flat without my permission!" he shouted. "Now, tell me where you were!"

When I hesitated, he flung me up against the wall, one hand around my neck. This routine was as familiar to me as cleaning my teeth and I knew, in the next instant, the other hand would punch me in the stomach. The stomach which housed my baby.

"Stop!" I shrieked. "I'm pregnant!"

The silence which followed was dangerous and loaded. This moment would, I knew, live always in my consciousness. I had admitted I was pregnant. I had accepted I was pregnant. In my first task as a mother, I had protected my baby from harm. I had done something right, at last. I knew, then, that nobody would ever hurt my baby. My maternal instinct burned brightly, and it was stronger, far stronger, than my own sense of self-preservation. This was not about me. It was about my baby. And things would be very different from now on.

When Nigel released his grip, I fell to the floor, and he kicked me to the side of the face several times. I was in agony. But my baby was safe.

"You'll have to get rid of it," he said. "Take some tablets."

Staggering to my feet, I shook my head.

"No," I replied firmly. "I'm not going to let my baby down. That's what you and Mum did to me. I'm keeping it and I will bring it up myself."

Nigel was visibly shocked, but not as shocked as I was. I could not believe this change in my character. Even my voice was different. Nigel paced the room, his fists bunched.

"It will be a vegetable," he said spitefully. "You're carrying a disabled kid. You need an abortion. I'll book you in at a clinic."

His words sent a tremor through me, but I stood firm.

"I don't care," I retorted. "I'm having the baby."

"You can't!" he yelled. "We're biologically related. The baby will be a vegetable!"

Normally, I'd have been petrified. But instead, a calm, like a warm blanket, settled on me. Suddenly I saw a reason for the trauma. I saw a point to it all. I had suffered in order for my baby to thrive. I had learned how not to be from my own parents and my first test as a mother was happening right now.

"You'd better not do a DNA test," he seethed. "If you do, I will kill you. In fact, I could kill you now, Lou-Lou. Just get rid of you and nobody would ever know. I could bury you in the yard out the back.

"And you know, I have access to insulin pens. I'm good friends with a diabetic. I could inject you whilst you're asleep. I could kill you so easily."

My teeth were chattering with fear, but I couldn't let this go. I had to show him things were different now.

"I saw the doctor today and I'm booked in for another appointment next week," I lied. "I have an appointment with the midwife as well. They have my name and address. They know I'm from Oldham. They have Mum's address. So if you hurt me, they will find out. They will come looking for me."

Dizzy with the elation of standing up for myself for the first time, I marched up to my room. I had gone from wounded to warrior. From beaten to battler. From victim to survivor. It was the most complete metamorphosis, for at last, I had found my purpose. Like a butterfly, emerging from the chrysalis, I was ready to fly.

Late at night, Nigel appeared in the doorway, a hulking shadow set against the light of the landing. Swearing, he threw more tablets at me.

"These will get rid of the problem," he shouted.

I had no idea whether he was referring to me, or the baby, or both of us. But I no longer cared what he said. I just needed to get out of here.

22

THE NEXT morning, I was expecting more arguments. But Nigel greeted me with a creepy smile and said, "I was thinking we might go for a drive, Lou-Lou. See, I've had an idea."

I listened, my insides curling in disgust, as he suggested a second viewing of the show-home.

"We can bring the baby up there, me and you together," he said. "Our own little family. There's a box room for the baby. A spare room for Maisie to stay over. And the double bedroom for us."

"What?" I asked, stunned. "Are you serious?"

"You and me and our own baby," he explained. "It's the most natural thing in the world. Think about it, Stace. Nobody knows us round there. We could start again, as a couple."

Even from him, it was a deranged idea.

"You are my biological father," I reminded him. "You are not my boyfriend."

I shuddered as he slipped his arm around me and said, "I've got it all worked out, Stace. I'm one step ahead. You can bring up the baby while I launch the juice business. You need me, remember that. It's all going to be okay."

My mind was reeling, but I realised it was pointless to keep arguing with him. I needed to play him at his own game. Two days later, he announced he was nipping out for a while. As soon as his car drove away, I called the police from his spare mobile phone.

"I don't have long," I told the officer. "And I can't meet you here. It's too dangerous."

Instead, I arranged to meet him in a Sainsbury's café nearby. Hurrying out, I left the front door on the latch and made my way there. Even as I took my seat, I couldn't quite believe where my sudden change of character had come from. For six months I'd tried and failed to pluck up the courage to speak to the police, and now, finally, here I was. It felt as though the baby was sending me waves of strength, sharing her courage with me.

"My biological father is violent to me," I said. "I'm terrified of him."

From the attack a few days earlier, I had bruises down the side of my face and a line of fingerprints around my neck. The officer took photos.

"I'd like to come to your home," he said. "We need to speak to your father."

But I shook my head. I wasn't about to put myself in more danger than I was already. I didn't tell him I was pregnant either. My experience with social services made me wary and I was worried they might take my baby away the moment it was born.

"How can I help you then?" he asked.

"Please call my mum," I said. "She mustn't tell Nigel. But please tell her I'm in danger and I need to get back to Oldham."

It was a risk. But walking back to the flat, I felt better that now someone knew I was in trouble. Someone was on my side. Speaking to the police made me feel alive. It was the start of my fight back. I managed to get to the flat before Nigel and when he returned, he seemed in a better mood.

"I've got a plan," I told him. "I need to go back to Oldham to have the baby and then I'll come back, when it's born, and we can live in the showhouse."

Nigel frowned.

"If I stay here, people will quickly work out the baby is yours," I explained. "I already told the doctor and midwife that I live with my dad. It's in my medical records now. If you start pretending to be my partner, they'll be suspicious, and you will end up in jail."

Nigel snorted.

"Never," he scoffed. "They'll never put me behind bars. Maybe you need to get rid of the baby instead. Get an abortion."

His words lit a fire within me.

"That will never happen," I vowed. "This is my baby and I'm keeping it."

Maybe Nigel was taken aback by the change in me, or worried that I might spill the beans to a midwife or a doctor. Because he said, "How do I know you'll come back when the baby is born?"

I held out my palms towards him and tried to smile.

"Like you said, I need you. I have no money and I have nowhere to live. Mum will have me back for a few months, but I can't stay there forever. I can't manage on my own."

Nigel thought for a while and then he said, "Okay. You can go back to Oldham on condition you stick to my story. You will tell everyone you met a bloke on a motorbike at Southend Airshow, and you disappeared with him overnight. When you came home, you found out you were pregnant.

"He's the father of the baby. His name is…"

He looked around him for inspiration and at that moment, there was a clip of the England footballers John Terry and Scott Carson on TV.

"His name is John Carson," he said triumphantly. "You got that?"

Soberly, I nodded. But inside, I was punching the air. Jumping up and down in celebration. This was it! He was going to let me go!

"Now, you tell anyone I'm the father and I'll come to Oldham and kill you." he hissed, pushing his face right into mine, so I could see those awful nose hairs quivering.

"You have a DNA analysis, and I'll kill you. Got it?"

I nodded again.

"Here's your first test," he said, dialling Mum's number and handing me his phone.

When Mum answered, I explained, quietly and carefully, that I had met a man at Southend Air show named John Carson and was pregnant.

218

"Please can I come home?" I asked.

I hoped, by now, she'd heard from the police officer. But with Nigel towering over me, I also hoped she wouldn't mention it. Mum sounded shocked, but said, "Yes, no problem, Stace. I didn't send a birthday present for you, so I'll send money for your coach ticket."

She also sent a little extra for a new suitcase. The next few days dragged, and I flipped constantly between my excitement at leaving and worry that Nigel might change his mind. Even when I was packed and ready to go, on June 22, I still feared he might stop me.

"And you'll be back, with the baby, to live in the showhouse," he checked, as I pulled my case out on the pavement. "You must never leave me, Stace. You must come back."

"Yes," I replied. "I promise. I'm looking forward to it."

I didn't understand why he would ever believe I would agree to that. But then, I didn't understand the way his mind worked at all and neither did I want to. He handed me his spare mobile phone, fully charged, so we could keep in touch, and insisted on walking to Southend train station with me. He made me carry my own bag and, on the platform, he leaned in close, so that his lips brushed my ear. For a stomach-churning moment, I thought he was going to kiss me. Instead, he whispered, "I have given you something which nobody else can, Lou-Lou. Never forget that."

Then he pressed his lips even closer, so that they were suckered onto my ear, and hissed, "If you breathe a word to anyone, I will find out and I will kill you and I will kill the baby. Always remember, Lou-Lou, I will follow you through your life and I will always know where you are. I am one step ahead of you."

23

STEPPING OFF the bus in Oldham was like stepping out of hell. I had made it. My legs buckled with sheer emotion as I gulped in fresh air, like I was breathing unaided for the first time. In that moment, I realised my baby and I had saved each other; she was my lifeline as I was hers. We had got out of there together. Looking to my right, I spotted Mum waving.

"Hey Stace!" she called. "Here, let me take that suitcase."

On our way home, she chatted away, asking about my journey and my time in Southend. She mentioned our chats on MSN and I worked out Nigel must have been messaging her, pretending to be me. I noticed, vaguely, that she was far more animated than usual, but I was too busy savouring my escape to think any more of it. Then she said, "So, what about the baby? Can I ask about the father? Is he going to help you, Stace?"

And in that moment, my bubble popped and the enormity of what I was facing smashed me in the face, as though I'd been hit with a concrete block.

"I don't want to talk about it," I mumbled.

The credits were rolling on the horror film I had left behind – but the sequel was already taking shape. How was I going to manage? I was 18 years old, carrying my biological father's baby, with nobody to confide in. I blinkered my eyes with my hands, as though I could shut the world out. But I could not shut Nigel out. Moments later, his phone bleeped inside my pocket.

Hey, Lou-Lou. Just checking you arrived safe. Miss you x

I gulped back tears and Mum, presuming I was upset over the mythical John Carson, squeezed my hand and said, "You're not on your own. You've got me. I'll help as much as I can, Stace."

I was desperate to tell her the truth, desperate for someone to share my burden. But I remembered Nigel's threat to kill me and my baby, and I knew I had to keep quiet. Mum had moved to a new place, and she had cleared out the bigger bedroom for me and the baby.

"I couldn't stay in the old house," she confided. "I kept thinking I could hear my baby crying. Losing Billy made me really ill. I had to try and start again."

I had my first ante-natal appointment the following week, which confirmed my baby was due February 1, 2008. I worked out I had fallen pregnant at that first attack on the eve of my 18th birthday. Shocked and sickened, I tried to bury the information. I knew I could not afford to dwell on the past.

"Can you tell at this stage if the baby is disabled?" I asked the midwife, anxiously. "I'm a bit worried about it."

She smiled.

"It's perfectly natural to worry about things at this stage," she replied. "You're a first-time mum so it's all brand new. But please try not to think about it. You're young and healthy, and your baby will be fine."

When I got home, Nigel sent another sickly message and I was glad when the battery eventually died, and he could no longer reach me. But as the weeks rolled by, my fear grew alongside my foetus. On the outside, I played the role of a committed young mum making textbook preparations for her new arrival. I gave up smoking and I didn't drink any alcohol. And my diet, for so long a source of distress, improved dramatically. I began eating sensible, balanced meals, and I snacked on fruit and vegetables. I even found I could manage salad, as long as it was served in separate portions on my plate. Mum laughed when she saw me nibbling at small, individual piles of tomato, cucumber and lettuce.

"It's good for the baby," I told her.

"You're really making an effort," she replied.

I painted my bedroom in light blue colours to prepare for my new arrival and began saving for equipment. I chose a top-of-the-range silver-cross pram, at a cost of over £400, which I could not afford, but I ordered it regardless. I was determined my baby would have the very best of everything. Maybe I desperately hoped that I could compensate for her dysfunctional background by indulging her materially.

"I'll pay half," Mum offered. "In fact, I'll go halves on everything with you."

The transformation in my mother was quite remarkable. But I was locked so tightly in my own private world of despair that I barely considered it.

As my stomach swelled, so did my anxiety, red and angry like an inflamed boil in my brain. I had ghoulish nightmares where my baby was born without a head, or without limbs. In one recurring dream, the baby was already in a wheelchair when she was delivered. In another, I gave birth to a child without any bones, and so she simply folded flat, like a sheet of paper, when she was laid in my arms. I woke, breathless and sweating, my heart hammering with panic. What if Nigel was right? What if I was carrying a baby with such severe disabilities that she did not even survive? My bump bloomed and I tried in vain to count the fingers and toes, worrying there were some missing. Nigel's warnings constantly swarmed around my brain like wasps.

The kid will be disabled. The kid will be a vegetable.

Just remembering his voice made me feel dirty and grimy, and I took four or five baths a day. But no matter how much soap and shower gel I used, I could not wash this away. At each ante-natal appointment, I pleaded for further tests and reassurance that my baby was okay.

"Do you have a family history of problems?" the midwife asked. "I don't understand your preoccupation with disabilities."

I shook my head miserably. How could I possibly begin to explain the trigger for this obsession?

"So, what is it then?" she asked.

I yearned to confide in her, but Nigel's threat rang as loudly in my ear as if he were sitting right next to me. Besides, even if he didn't manage to kill me, I was certain social services would take my baby away when they found out who the father was. I did not feel they had helped me in the past and I could not count on them in the future either. My 24-week scan showed I was carrying a little girl and Mum burst into tears of joy. But I was consumed with making sure all the checks had been done correctly.

"Are you sure she's okay?" I pressed. "What about her head? Does it look normal to you?"

A few weeks later, at the clinic, the midwife said, "Oh, the baby is measuring a little bigger than we'd expect."

I shot up from the trolley in alarm.

"Is she disabled?" I shrieked. "What's wrong with her?"

The midwife smiled.

"No, of course not," she replied. "She's just a little bigger than average. Everything seems fine."

But I was not convinced. I was tormented by thoughts that dragged me nearer and nearer to the edge of the darkest crater and I wasn't sure how much more I could take. Was I being selfish, giving birth to this baby? Should I have had the termination that Nigel had tried to force upon me? I wanted my baby, no matter whether or not she was disabled. But was I being fair to her?

As I tortured myself, the incompatibilities crawled in and out of my mind. My baby was also my father's baby. My own child would be my half-sibling, and his child would be his grandchild too. The stress of carrying this around, and carrying it alone, was paralysing. Some days, I was only just out of the bath when I started running another. I could not get clean. For it was mental, not physical hygiene, which I craved, and there was no solution for that.

Aside from attending ante-natal appointments, I rarely left the house. I froze when people referred to my baby or asked about the father. Mum did not press me, perhaps she felt I would confide in her when I was ready. After Christmas, she helped me pack my hospital bag and we began preparing for the birth. By now, I weighed 13 stone, I had gained an incredible five stone during pregnancy, eating more in those nine months than I had in the previous 17 years! I had constant, nagging back pain and I was becoming uncomfortable and grouchy.

"Let's do a jigsaw," Mum suggested. "Just like the old days."

There was some solace and peace in poring over thousand-piece jigsaws, and more than that, I loved the closeness with Mum. Our bond had grown and strengthened since I'd moved back to live with her, she hadn't missed a single scan or appointment at the hospital. She was there to rub my swollen ankles and soothe my fears. She seemed so excited about the baby. Mum was trying, I was trying. Our relationship was in smithereens but slowly, like a jigsaw, we were piecing it together. Some parts may be beyond repair. But I was beginning to believe that it could be, not rebuilt, but built for the first time.

Mum was wrong about one thing though – this was nothing like the old days. Nothing at all.

* * * *

My due date came and went without so much as a twinge, and I took the lack of activity as a sure sign that something was wrong with my baby.

"Everything's fine," Mum told me. "Stop stressing. Not many babies are born on time."

But I couldn't help it. I was convinced the baby was so disabled that normal labour would not be possible. I worried I was putting her through unbearable pain, simply by giving birth to her.

"Why not try a hot bath?" Mum suggested. "Try and relax."

With that, I had a grotesque flashback to Nigel climbing into the bath with me and I shivered.

"Well how about a hot curry?" she said. "Might set you off."

Now I was remembering Nigel cooking chicken curry, setting the table with candles and flowers, as though it was a date night. I battled against the need to retch.

"No," I muttered. "I don't think so."

The attacks played over and over in my mind on a loop. Like Nigel's mix tape, I could not bear the repetition.

Three days after my due date, I relented and ran a hot bath. Early the next morning, at 4.40am, my contractions began. Mum came with me to the Royal Oldham Hospital and squeezed my hand.

"I'm here," she said. "You're going to be alright."

But when the midwife pulled back the sheet to examine

me, I pulled back in terror. I could feel Nigel's weight again, so substantial and heavy that my lungs felt flattened and drained of air.

"Just relax," she said briskly, snapping on her gloves. "We've a long way to go."

She could not have known what I had been through and nor could I have confided in her. Over the next 12 hours, I tried every pain relief on offer. I seemed to be stuck in 30-minute cycles of 10 minutes laughing, 10 minutes wailing and 10 minutes shouting. Though I enjoyed the laughing, it wasn't getting me anywhere. Eventually, after an epidural and some further intervention, my baby girl was born at 4.20pm on February 4 2008, weighing 8lbs.

"Is she okay?" I gasped. "Is she disabled? Please tell me?"

It seemed an age before a midwife replied, and in that moment all my fears, worries and paranoias collided with one big smash.

"She's absolutely perfect!" she beamed. "Here Mum, have your first cuddle."

"No!" I said instinctively. "I can't do it!"

"Don't be silly," she smiled.

I felt a warm body on my chest and, as I dared to open my eyes, I felt a rush of pure joy, a dazzling starburst of happiness. From gritty, murky, beginnings I had been gifted a shimmering pearl. A gem more precious than all the crown jewels. After years of grey misery, the colour flooded back into my world. Ever since my tournament victory, aged 12, I'd been searching to replicate that euphoria, that all-consuming flood of joy. I had thought I would never find it again. But now, as my baby daughter stared at me, wide-eyed and wise, I felt it. Only this time, I knew, it was here to last.

"Welcome baby girl," I murmured. "Nobody will ever hurt you. I promise."

We had only a brief cuddle before I was whisked down to theatre to be stitched. And the moment she was lifted out of my arms, panic set in once again. Even as I was wheeled down the corridor, my mind whirred like a concrete mixer of worry. Had they counted all her toes? Had they checked her vision? What if one leg was shorter than the other?

"Can you please check my baby again?" I begged. "I think she might be disabled. I think there's something wrong."

Later, when I came round from the anaesthetic, I spotted the tiny cot at the side of my bed, and there she was. A baby. My baby. The shock rippled right through me, it was almost too big for me to comprehend. All through the pregnancy, I had been so focused on her having a disability that I had not considered the how and why of her existence.

Confronting it head on, I felt suddenly out of my depth. Not for the first time, the size of the task ahead felt too big. How would I cope? What would I tell her? I marvelled at this little being, so beautiful, so precious, something so unbelievably pure which had come from something so absolutely rotten.

But how could I be a good mother when there were glaring, gaping wounds in my own childhood? I decided to call her Kadie Jade, using the initials of my grandparents Ken and Joan. Three days on it was Mum's birthday and I was allowed to go home.

"This is the best birthday ever," she smiled. "I am so proud of you, Stace."

She fussed and cooed over Kadie, doting on her with a devotion I found both endearing and staggering. Ever since I'd arrived back in Oldham, Mum had been so kind to me. And now, with Kadie, she could not do enough. Conflicted, I didn't know how to feel. One minute, I resented that I had missed out on this, the next, I was grateful she was there for her granddaughter in a way she had not been there for me. One reason for the change in Mum was that she'd finally had support following the loss of her baby boy, Billy. She had, I realised, been badly traumatised by his death.

A second factor was she was no longer bullied or ruled by the people around her. Her relationship with Karl was on-off and slowly fizzling out, and his friends were nowhere to be seen. Allowed to blossom on her own, Mum was a completely different person. Again, my feelings were splintered. I was pleased she was happy, grateful she was there for Kadie. But nothing could compensate for those years when I felt she had let me down.

"Did your Dad send a baby card?" Mum asked, as she flicked through the cards on the mantelpiece. "I haven't seen one."

"Me neither," I mumbled.

"And what about John Carson?" she asked. "Has he been in touch?"

Again, I mumbled a reply, and Mum must have sensed my discomfort, because she said, "When you're ready to talk love, I'm here."

Nigel had not been in contact since those early messages on his spare mobile phone, which I had since thrown away. It should have been a relief, but for me, no news was bad news. He must surely, by now, have worked out that I'd had the baby. What was he plotting? What was he planning? I was convinced he was coming for me. Worse, he was coming for Kadie, too.

24

IN THOSE early days, I clung to Kadie as though we were magnetised.

"You two are joined at the hip," Mum smiled. "You never put her down, Stace."

I was still convinced the hospital had missed something and that she would be diagnosed as disabled in some way. I would, of course, have loved her regardless, but in my mind it was a link with Nigel, and I didn't want him to influence her life in any way. When the health visitor came, she remarked that Kadie's top lip was protruding a little over the bottom one.

"She just needs a dummy, it will fix itself," she said.

"Are you sure?" I demanded. "Are you sure that's all it is? Could it be something more serious?"

But the health visitor was right and, in a week or two, the problem vanished. So I just redirected my anxieties elsewhere. I told myself I did not deserve this perfect baby and that she would be taken from me, one way or another. She slept with her fingers curled around mine through the bars of her cot, so I could be as close to her as possible. I had a heart monitor under her mattress, a thermometer in the room, and baby monitors around the house. I was convinced someone, or something, would try to steal her from me. She was just too beautiful, too perfect, for the likes of me.

"Baby blues," Mum reassured me, when she caught me sobbing at the side of Kadie's cot. "It will pass, love."

I longed to tell her the truth, but the words clogged in my throat. How could I take that risk? I knew Nigel would come for me, I knew what he was capable of. Every night, I triple-checked the windows and doors. I jumped at every noise, every little creak and sigh of the walls and floors in the early hours. I rarely left the house in case he was lying in wait, just as he had all those years earlier, in the park. Although, as with every new baby, we had lots of visitors. Much as I tried to shut myself away, people wanted to come and admire the new arrival.

"Oh Stace, she's gorgeous," people said. "And she looks exactly like you. She has your brown eyes, doesn't she?"

I stretched my face into a smile. She had those dark eyes, just as I did. Just as he did. The physical similarities between us all were undeniable. But I wanted all memories of him gone. More than anything, I wanted to be a good mother. I loved this new role but could not believe how much motherhood weighed – the shame and fear, alongside the overwhelming responsibility. It was so heavy I was doubled over and folded in on myself. So many times, I did not feel strong enough to move forward. Yet at the same time, Kadie was my reason for doing so, she was my little miracle.

Though I refused to let Kadie out of my sight, there were times, paradoxically, when I could not bear to be near her. Bathing my baby daughter should have been one of the most cherished aspects of our daily routine. But for me, it had been sullied and spoiled beyond repair.

When bathtime came, my thoughts spiralled back to the attacks in the bathroom. I again saw Nigel climbing clumsily into my bathwater. I remembered his eyes travelling over my naked body. I could not possibly enjoy bathing my own daughter when my own experiences had been so grotesquely distorted.

Luckily, Mum was thrilled to do it and if she found my behaviour odd, she didn't say so. After Kadie was bathed, she handed her back to me, wrapped in a fluffy towel, and I breathed her in, the purity, the innocence, the trust. I hoped, with all my heart, that my love for my daughter could outshine the hatred I felt for my father.

＊＊＊＊

When Kadie was around six weeks old, I took her to see my foster mother, at the primary school. Pushing the pram through the gates, I felt an odd mix of pride and worry. I had dressed Kadie in a cute new outfit, with a matching hat. Her pram was brand-new and shiny. Her new changing bag swung on the hook. Her fluffy bunny lay tucked up in the pram, next to her. Somehow, I felt I had something to prove. I didn't feel good enough, I didn't feel like I made the grade, and that was why, aged 10, I had been taken away from them. In the school office, the staff cooed over Kadie's pram and my foster mother said, "She is so beautiful, Stace, and she looks just like you."

Though she fussed over Kadie, she didn't scoop her up for a cuddle, as I had hoped she might. I was only there for a few moments, and as we walked back to the bus stop, I felt wounded in a way that left me slightly stunned. I would far rather my foster mother had shunned me, than Kadie.

A couple of weeks later, I arranged to have Kadie christened. I was not especially religious, but I'd been sent to a religious school myself. I was copying everything my foster family had done, following their lead, because I had no other examples, and did not feel confident in my own abilities as a mother. I didn't know what to do, or how to be, and they were the best example I had. No matter I had been torn from them, aged 10, and my life had lunged out of all control. I yearned for the idyll of my early childhood, and I wanted to recreate that for Kadie. Unwrapping those early memories, I painted my childhood in unrealistically fond and flattering hues. Had it *really* been like that, or did I cling to those years more because I had nothing else to attach myself to? I could not be sure.

The very first christening invite I wrote was to the Robinsons. And even in the card, I tried to sell myself.

'I'm doing a bit of a party, lots of food and drinks,' I wrote. 'Would be lovely to see you all.'

It was as though I felt the offer of sandwiches and sausage rolls might swing it, if they would not come for me, perhaps they would come for the buffet. That I, alone, was not enough. But I thought back to the glass animals I'd bought for my mother, in an effort to win her affections. It hadn't worked then and deep down I knew it wouldn't work now.

The day of the christening dawned and, predictably, they did not come. I told myself I should be used to rejection, but this one really stung, as I felt it was directed at Kadie, as well as me.

"You've got me," I told her, as I carried her into church. "You've always got me."

In July 2008, when Kadie was five months old, I was offered my own house on a quiet street just a few minutes' walk from Mum's. There were two bedrooms, and a small back garden, and it was a perfect first-time home for a first-time mum. On the one hand, I was thrilled, Kadie and I needed our own place. But at the same time, I was terrified. I did not know how I was going to cope. Mum was so hands-on with Kadie, she bathed her every night, she paced the living room in the early hours when Kadie had colic, she bought little gifts and treats. But more than the practical help, I valued her support and reassurance. Simply, I valued her as a mother.

I arranged to leave Kadie with Mum for a week or two while I cleaned and decorated our new home. It was a genuine request, I didn't want Kadie inhaling the paint smells. But I also knew that I was pushing back the day when I would become responsible for her on my own. While Mum cared for Kadie, I painted a cream and chocolate combination on the walls downstairs. Upstairs, I decorated Kadie's room in a princess theme, painting the walls pink with stencils of castles and princesses. The only room I didn't decorate was my own. My only focus was my daughter. Mum popped in to admire my work and she said, "You'll be wanting Kadie to move in now then? I'll miss her so much."

"Could she stay with you a while longer?" I stuttered. "Just whilst I get things sorted here."

And so we fell into a stilted sort of routine. Kadie stayed with my mother, and I spent every day there with her. Parenting was the steepest of learning curves for me, I had no blueprint for how to look after a baby, no learned behaviours or past memories to rely on. Most parents raise a child by picking out the best parts from their own childhood and adding in more of their own. For me, it had to be a clean slate. All I had learned from my own parents was how not to be.

I heard one mother talk about the benefits of a soft play area called 'Cheeky Chimps' and so as soon as Kadie was sitting up on her own, I booked a session in the ball pool. I was grateful for the pointers, but at the same time my own confidence was further whittled away, because I didn't make any decisions for her myself. I didn't know what kind of mother I should be. I was obsessive about doing all her care myself, except when it came to bathing. I could not shake the impression that it was inappropriate for me to wash my own daughter.

In truth, I had no idea what was normal or appropriate. Friends told me they bathed with their babies, in the same water, and I was at once envious and repulsed. I wanted that closeness and that innocence, but it just did not feel right. Much as I tried to change it, I could not help the way I had been conditioned.

After Kadie was tucked up in her cot at Mum's, I went home each night on my own. Alone, in the early hours, I wrestled with my anxieties and inadequacies. What was wrong with me? My love for Kadie was so overwhelming, it left me feeling weak and crushed. It was as though by loving her, I was left depleted in some way. Surely it was not supposed to be this way. As a mother, I was supposed to grow outwardly, not shrivel back into myself.

Nigel had, by proxy, become a permanent fixture in my life. In trying to run from him when I was pregnant, I had unwittingly handed him a starring role in his own sick drama.

Each time I looked at Kadie, it was like looking at myself. But I became more conscious of the likeness between me and him, so I could no longer bear to even look at myself in the mirror. I hated the shape of my face and my athletic build, once a bonus, now became a curse. And his dark eyes, the keepers of so many secrets, well, I had those eyes too.

Kadie was an innocent child, a victim in all of this. I wanted to be a good parent. I wanted to give her the kind of childhood I'd never had. But constantly fighting a riptide of emotions was so much tougher than I could ever have imagined.

Motherhood was my greatest gift. But it was also my greatest challenge.

* * * *

By Kadie's first Christmas, she had not spent a single night in her new princess bedroom. I either returned home late in the evening, or I stayed with her at Mum's. On the nights I was alone in my new house, I tortured myself with accusations and recriminations. What kind of mother was I? To dull my inner voices, I began drinking heavily, but the more I drank, the worse I felt. If Mum picked up on my anguish, she never spoke about it.

Once, she said to me, "You know Stace, you never mention John Carson. You never talk about Kadie's dad."

The silence which followed stretched out like a taut elastic between us.

"I'm sure you'll tell me when you're ready," she said, patting my knee, and I was grateful she did not pull any further. Any more pressure and I might have snapped completely.

Kadie's first birthday came, and we planned a party at Mum's house. I couldn't help feeling a fraud as I hung banners and blew up balloons. What kind of mother did not take her own child home with her each night? What kind of daughter gave birth to her own father's child? I shovelled blame onto myself, until I was almost buried by it. Again, I thought of the sand mountain, a tomb in my mind. And I thought of Nigel.

All through the party, I was on tenterhooks, convinced he was about to make an appearance. As the music began for *Pass The Parcel*, I moved to the window to check the street. I could not relax. As the guests left, a relative pulled me aside and said, "Why don't you think of leaving Kadie with your mum, full-time? Might be better for all of you. You were in foster care when you were small too, weren't you?"

It was like a punch to the gut. But as I struggled to find a reply, I had a sudden moment of absolute clarity. His words, whether well-meaning or spiteful, shone a harsh and unforgiving light onto the parallels between my childhood and Kadie's. How could I have been so thoughtless, so selfish? I would not allow history to repeat itself, nor for my own sufferings to be heaped upon my baby daughter.

"I'm taking Kadie home with me tonight, Mum, if that's okay," I announced. "It's time we started the next chapter."

And from that day, I never looked back.

We quickly slotted into a routine, visiting Mum most days, but always returning home. In the living room, I had a bookcase stacked with toys and baby books. We had a ball pit and a paddling pool in the back garden.

As soon as Kadie could toddle about, I set about teaching her to play football, trying to quell my own competitive spirit when she picked the ball up and popped it under her arm.

"Not like that, Kadie," I spluttered.

"Yes, like that," she retorted, and I could see, already, she was more than a match for me.

Scooping her into my arms, just feeling the warmth of her cheek against mine, made my heart sing with happiness. I loved watching her grow, seeing her develop as a person in her own right. She was not me. She was not him. She was quite simply herself.

Once Kadie was settled in her new home, I enrolled at college to re-sit Maths and English, I joined a football team, and I found a nursery for Kadie. Even though I was still only 20 years old, I knew I would never have another child.

Nigel's words often returned to haunt me: *Always remember I have given you something nobody else can.*

Standing on the platform in Southend, I had not realised the significance of that statement. But now I realised I could never consider having another child in a normal relationship, because it would push Kadie out. She would feel like an outcast and I knew from bitter experience how that felt. I was robbed of having more children. And Kadie would grow up without siblings. By having Kadie, I had handed Nigel control over my life forever and his poisonous legacy followed me like a cloud.

I did not regret a thing, but as an only child, I knew it was important for Kadie to mix with other kids at nursery. It was also a big step for me to leave her in the care of strangers. I ruled out local nurseries, thinking they would be high on Nigel's list if he tried to kidnap her. Instead, I booked her in at a nursery in the countryside beyond Oldham. We needed two buses to get there, but I felt better knowing she was hidden away.

Handing her over to the nursery staff filled me with a peculiar mix of terror and relief. This was all part of my attempt to be a normal mother, but the stress was debilitating.

On the surface, life was organised and smooth, yet beneath the waterline, like a swan, I was paddling madly, desperate to stay afloat. Being a mother was, much of the time, like being trapped in a whirlpool and the more I struggled, the deeper it sucked me in. Towards the end of 2009, the health visitor dropped in for a visit.

"I have a few concerns," she said.

"About what?" I asked, my skin tightening with apprehension.

"Not about Kadie," she reassured me. "Kadie is well looked after and well loved. You are an excellent mother. My concerns are not for Kadie. They are for you, Stace."

She looked me straight in the eye and for a horrible moment, I worried I might crumble. But I straightened myself and snapped, "Well, I don't need your concern. Thank you."

When she had gone, I slid down the back of the door and sobbed. How much longer could I keep this up? In trying to find myself, I was losing myself completely.

25

IN DECEMBER 2009, Kadie and I wrapped up warm and went to play in the garden. We had only been outside a few minutes when she fell off her slide and banged her head. She seemed fine in herself, but like all mums, I felt terrible.

At nursery the next morning, I was anxious to point the bruise out to a staff member, but it was Christmas panto day, and the place was chaotic. Her keyworker was nowhere to be seen.

A few days later, I was collecting her from nursery when another staff member said, "Kadie has picked nits up. It's going round the whole class, most of her friends have them too."

I started to say I'd pick up a bottle of nit shampoo on my way home. But then she continued, "Oh, don't worry, we've already bathed her and washed her hair."

My jaw slackened in shock.

"You did what?" I spluttered. "You had no right to bathe my child! None at all!"

I could hear my voice rising to an unreasonable level. In my hysteria, I was convinced this was part of a plan to abuse her. Why else would they bathe her without my consent? Why else would they take all her clothes off without me there to supervise? The nursery staff seemed stunned at my outburst which only incensed me further. Then one asked, "Is this connected to the bruise on Kadie's head?"

With a thud, I realised they thought I didn't want her bathed because I was covering up her bruise. This was going from bad to worse. In anguish, I fell to my knees and sobbed.

"This has nothing to do with her bruise," I wept. "You have no idea what has happened to me and why you shouldn't bathe her. None at all."

The nursery manager did her best to calm me down, before she brought Kadie out of the classroom. Back at home, as logic settled, I realised how appallingly I had over-reacted. I was transferring my own trauma, my own mistrust, onto the very people who were looking after my daughter and keeping her safe. Flushed with remorse, I relived my temper tantrum, and my thoughts wound straight back to Nigel. I had combusted, just like him. I had his build, his eyes, his face. Now I had his temper. Why was I turning into the very thing I despised the most?

That night, after Kadie went to bed, I raked over past memories, paralysed again by fear and shame. Scrolling through social media, it didn't take me long to find Nigel's account. Perhaps, subconsciously, I knew what I would find. Perhaps, subconsciously, I knew what I had to do. Clicking on a photo of him with two girls, one a teenager, one a toddler, I expected to explode in panic. Instead, at my core,

I felt a cold, calm confidence. Picking up the phone, I dialled 999 and said, "I need to report an attack ."

An officer came to my home the next day and after a long chat, she made arrangements for me to give a video interview at the police station. Saying it out loud was the biggest gamble I had ever taken. But it was also a huge catharsis. By keeping my secret I was rotting from the inside out. My silence was allowing Nigel's hold to continue and strengthen day by day. Deep down I had known all along that he could not be allowed to get away with this. I could not allow him to go free, to abuse again. I had told myself I was staying quiet for Kadie's sake. Now I realised it was precisely for her sake, and for all other girls, that I had to speak out.

"We'll be in touch," the officers promised. "It's likely that we'll need DNA samples if he denies it."

"Oh, he will definitely deny it," I said grimly.

After Nigel was arrested, I went onto high alert, convincing myself he was waiting round every street corner, hiding behind every parked car. I became so afraid that I dropped out of college and took Kadie out of nursery. We bunkered down, like fugitives, at home. It was the only way I could keep her safe.

As expected, officers came to the house to take a DNA swab from my mouth, and Kadie's too.

"We also need a DNA swab from your biological mother," they said.

I couldn't warn Mum in advance, because I couldn't bear to have the conversation. And even after she had given the sample, she did not raise the issue with me. Some weeks later, as we were playing with Kadie in her ball pit, Mum said casually, "So, I spoke with the police."

She threw a ball up in the air to make Kadie laugh, ending the conversation before I could shut it down myself. I was guarded, as she was, and neither of us wanted to talk about it.

I went through the whole police process on my own, in a strange and lonely bubble. Part of me wished Mum would put her arms around me, but if I was honest, I could not have accepted the gesture. I just was not ready for that. Waiting for the results, I drove myself mad with worry. What if they came back negative? What if there was a mistake in the lab? He would definitely come for me and kill me. The worries chased round and round my head and infected my dreams too.

In one nightmare, Nigel barged into my house, and I pulled Kadie behind the sofa to hide. When his leering face appeared over the back of the sofa, I braced myself, believing I was about to die. Instead, he plucked Kadie from my arms and left with her.

Waking, sweating and sobbing, I realised losing Kadie would be the very definition of a fate worse than death. I would die before I let him ruin her, the way he had ruined me.

In those weeks, whilst the tests were taking place, there was no help or advice. I had no support from the police, or any connected organisations, to reassure me that my misgivings were to be expected. Six weeks after the DNA swabs were taken, I took a call from the police at Mum's house.

"It's a match," said the officer. "We're going to charge him."

Sinking to my knees, I felt no joy. Only a determination and a responsibility to see this through.

26

AS I waited for a trial date, I plucked up courage to ask Mum about my early years. I couldn't bear any more secrets.

"I'll tell you what I can," she said. "But there's so much I don't know. And it's going to hurt you, Stace."

She explained I had been taken into care as a toddler because she could no longer look after me. I had suspected as much, but the truth was hard to hear. Previously, aged 18 months, I had suffered a fracture to my leg, bite marks to my face and bruising. I had to accept I would never know for sure how or why they had occurred. Some pieces of the jigsaw would be missing forever, just like the charity shop bargains Grandad had bought when I was small.

But with each revelation, images of my childhood built up like a slowly developing Polaroid. Mum confirmed that both she and my foster parents had applied to the courts for me to live with them. My eyes misted over with tears as I realised the Robinsons really had wanted me to stay with them. But the court had ruled in favour of my mother, and so I was sent to live with her. How different my life would have been, if only those officials had allowed me to remain where I was happiest. Nigel had applied to the court to have contact with me, which was why the social worker had taken me to see him. Eventually, of course, I had lived with him full-time. My heart cried for the lost little girl I had once been, shipped between these households, neither of whom wanted me, nor was fit to care for a child.

"I appreciate you telling me this," I told Mum, and we shared a hug. "You're right, it does hurt. But I need to hear it."

There was far worse to come.

I contacted other family members, and the scraps of information I was given left me dumbfounded. After the attackss, I had believed nothing could ever shock me again. But I was wrong. In disbelief, I checked the information with Oldham Magistrates' Court, hoping against hope that it was nothing more than rumour. But officials later confirmed that when I was just eight months old, Nigel had been convicted of: 'unlawful sexual intercourse with a girl (aged) 13 years.' He was 21 years old at the time and sentenced to a period of probation.

He had done it before. Every bone in my body screamed out. Fury, like molten lava, bubbled at the back of my throat. Why had he been granted contact with me, through social services? Why had I been allowed to stay with him, unsupervised, time after time throughout my childhood? Why had nobody – not a single soul – stepped in to save me?

I had believed the attacks in Southend were out of the blue, a shocking aberration which could not have been predicted. But no. The authorities knew – everyone knew – that Nigel Taylor had been convicted of a sexual offence against a child many years before he began his abuse of me. I had not simply slipped through the system, I had been actively shoved to one side, trampled and squashed by the very people who should have been there to help me.

The pain was physical, cramping through me until I vomited. And yet, parallel to the shock and the hurt was a renewed sense of purpose. He had been allowed to reoffend. He had been allowed to abuse me. But it would go no further. I would make sure of it.

"This stops with me," I said grimly. "He can't do this to another child."

One night, I wrote to my foster mother, telling her the grim facts about my stay in Southend and the forthcoming court case. Taking my letter, I went to the school where she worked, but found a new entry system was in place. There were new staff there, too, who didn't recognise me, so I had to wait outside the main doors. My foster mother popped her head outside briefly and took my letter. We exchanged a few meaningless pleasantries until I pretended that I had to rush off.

In the days afterwards, I braced myself for a reaction. I didn't want pity or sympathy. I just wanted to be acknowledged and loved. In the end, it was worse than I could ever have imagined, because there was no reaction at all. I had no response to my letter. These were the people who had picked me up, every time I had fallen as a child. Was it too much to expect they might pick me up once again?

Early in 2011, I received notification that Nigel Taylor would stand trial at Basildon Crown Court.

The officers in Oldham had shown me briefly around Oldham Magistrates Court, but it could not have prepared me for the terror of walking into a crown court for the first time in my life. The night before, Mum and I had travelled down together. In the tiny bathroom of the Travelodge, I had hacked off all my long hair and I had packed baggy, scruffy clothes to wear.

"Don't you have anything smart?" Mum frowned.

"No," I said flatly.

I did not want to be attractive to Nigel in any way. Besides, I could not bear to wear anything other than a tracksuit. In the foyer, the barrister introduced herself and ushered us into a side room. My legs buckled as I stumbled through the door. Now that the moment was here, I was so scared.

"You're welcome to go upstairs to the café to get a drink," she said. "But I must warn you that Nigel Taylor is in there too."

It did not seem fair, him having the run of the café, me imprisoned in a small room. But then, that was how it had always been, Nigel in control. If I had hoped the justice system would change that, then I was wrong.

Remember Lou-Lou, I am one step ahead.

The barrister leafed quickly through the paperwork and said, "He is going to be convicted on the DNA evidence. It makes no sense to go to trial. I will see if we can come to an agreement."

Mum and I spent four hours in the little room, too afraid

even to pop out to the loo, in case we bumped into Nigel. Eventually, the barrister returned, saying, "Good news, he will plead guilty to count two, sexual activity with a female child family member. He had no choice really. The DNA evidence is conclusive."

Relief trickled through me. I did not have to give evidence after all. The barrister disappeared again and when she came back, she announced Nigel had been sentenced to seven years in jail. Mum whooped in celebration; the barrister beamed widely. But I felt flat, like a popped football. Seven years? Was that really enough for what he had put me through? Seven hundred years, seven thousand, would not have been enough.

In a daze I left the court, and it was only in the days afterwards that I remembered he had also been charged with rape. This charge had been left to lie on file, because there had been no trial. I worked out his guilty plea to the second charge had been a kind of deal, a cost-cutting exercise to save the expense of a trial. My case was ticked off the list, so the next one could be heard.

And though I had felt great relief at the time, afterwards, I felt cheated. I wanted Nigel to face both charges. I wanted to have my say in court and to have the truth exposed at last. But though I was the victim, I was fast learning this process was not about me at all.

Back at home, I contacted Manchester Rape Crisis, who installed panic alarms in my home and offered me counselling.

"If he was jailed for seven years, he will probably only serve three and a half," they told me.

Shocked, I readjusted my timescale again. Then, at the end of that same year, I was warned he was being considered for day release to visit a family member. The length of his punishment was shrinking, and with it, my anxiety was growing. Each day was like a notch on an egg-timer; every grain of sand, every minute that passed, bringing me nearer and nearer to his release.

At the end of 2011, I received a £16,500 payout from the Criminal Injuries Compensation Authority. I had thought, after making the application, that the money would make me feel better in some way. But when it landed in my bank account, it felt like a stone around my neck. I'd never had so much money in my life, yet when I checked my balance, I felt sick with disgust. It almost felt like a gift from Nigel.

Anxious to get rid of it as quickly as possible, I began spending. It was December and so I gave Kadie a Christmas to remember. I bought her a trampoline, a bike and a toy kitchen. I bought a new wardrobe and a fridge freezer too. But every time I looked at them, I thought of him. I felt, irrationally, as though I was letting him back into my life. Within a year, I'd donated the wardrobe and the fridge freezer to a homeless charity, and I bought second-hand ones instead. Looking back, older and wiser, I wish I'd invested the money and used it for future counselling for Kadie and me.

Instead, it was all gone by the start of 2012.

* * * *

Kadie grew into a real live wire, who enjoyed taking stuff

apart and then trying, (not always successfully!), to put it back together.

One day, she was in love with Hello Kitty. The next, it was Spiderman. She was a whirlwind of energy and enthusiasm. I signed her up for acting lessons and Mum, 'Ninny' to Kadie, took her to dance classes. It was no surprise that she was already sick of football by the time she turned four. I'd put her off! In the evenings, we'd snuggle on the sofa to watch: *In the Night Garden* together. Kadie would usually doze in my arms, but the minute she heard the opening music, she'd spring up straight and start to clap. Every night, tucking her into bed I'd tell her, "Love you, Kades."

My heart bloomed with joy as she lisped, "Love you, Mamma."

We played a 'Love you, Love you more' game which sometimes lasted until I was on the landing and making my way downstairs.

"Love you more more more!" I heard her yell, as I reached the living room. Neither of us could bear to be the last one to say it.

Before Kadie was due to start school, the probation service arranged a meeting with the headteacher and the safeguarding team. They put security measures in place and asked for a photograph of Nigel. We agreed a password for anyone collecting Kadie from school. As we sat around the table, the probation officer said, "We need to bear in mind that Nigel Taylor will undergo rehabilitation. There is a possibility he might apply for access after he is released."

Like an angry tiger, I sprang to my feet, growling.

"There is no rehabilitation for what he did!" I shouted. "None. And he will never, ever have access to my daughter. He is a danger to all young girls."

This was one time I was not sorry I had lost my temper. I was appalled the probation officer could even suggest it. The system had let me down, and I had walked straight into the lion's den. I would not stand by and let the same thing happen to Kadie. Years later, that same probation officer came to my home with an apology. After meeting Nigel in person, he agreed that he was dangerous.

Kadie started school, and I felt so proud, her little hand in mine, as we walked into the schoolyard. She had a brand-new uniform, shoes, coat, bag and lunchbox. She had scented pencils, rubbers and felt pens in every colour. She had Hello Kitty wellies, an umbrella and a flowery sunhat. I knew what it was like to stand out through neglect. It was so important for me that Kadie fit in. But it wasn't long before she came home one day with a task to make a collage out of household rubbish.

"My teacher says get Mum and Dad to help," she announced with a frown. "So where is my Dad?"

My heart stuttered.

"You don't have a Dad," I said softly. "But you do have me. I'm both."

She seemed to accept that, quite happily, and I threw myself into collecting bottle tops and squares of tinfoil, ready for our collage. But the anxiety gnawed at the edges of my mind, eroding all chances of happiness. Constantly, I tried to recreate what I thought was the perfect childhood from my foster home, but always, I fell short. I felt I was not good enough. I was so critical of myself as a mother to the point where I focussed more on my faults than I did on actually being a mum. And was my time in foster care quite as idyllic as I would have myself believe? Because where was my family now?

I was modelling myself on parents who had virtually disowned me. And so, I strived constantly towards standards I could never attain, towards a Eutopia I could never reach. All I wanted for my daughter was the family I had never had. On my own, I felt I was not enough. And in trying to create this ideal environment, I was, in a cruel paradox, simply creating more anxiety.

At birthdays and Christmases, I over-compensated dramatically, saving all year round so that I could deluge Kadie with gifts. I suppose I hoped I could somehow distract her attention from the lack of family, from the lack of a father, by showering her with presents.

"You spoil her too much," people told me. "It's ridiculous."

The judgement just made me feel worse, which, in turn, made me determined to compensate Kadie even further. Besides, I was spending my own money. I never went out, I rarely drank or smoked. I was simply doing my best with what I had.

In October 2014, I was informed Nigel was due for release. It was no shock, I had been counting down the days for three and a half years, and he had squatted inside my head, all that time. Even so, I was on high alert, working myself into a frenzy, certain he would come to kill Kadie and me.

A previous occupant had run up a debt at my address and one day I opened the front door to find two bailiffs on the doorstep.

"I have no debts," I told them truthfully. "Leave me alone. This is nothing to do with me."

One of the men peered past me, into the hallway, where Kadie's pink bike and her toys were piled up. The way he eyed up her things sent a sudden bolt of electricity through me and with sickening clarity, I realised these were not bailiffs at all. They were kidnappers, sent by Nigel, to snatch my daughter. Screaming, I ran to my kitchen and grabbed a vegetable knife from the draining board.

"I will kill anyone who comes near my daughter," I screamed. "Leave us alone!"

It was only after the men had gone that my terror dissolved, and I realised I had grossly over-reacted. Just as at Kadie's nursery, when the staff had bathed her, I had lost all sense of reason. Was I turning into Nigel? No matter how I tried to control my temper, those angry genes somehow forced a way through. The bailiffs called the police over my threats, and I admitted everything. I felt so ashamed. Again, I was failing as a mother, letting myself and Kadie down.

The days passed, and there was no word from Nigel. But his release dominated my thoughts. He was like a parasite, living inside my brain and leeching my strength. One afternoon, Kadie pinched my mobile phone and hid it under a cushion.

"Have you seen my phone?" I asked, and she shook her head solemnly.

"No, Mummy," she replied. "I saw you with it upstairs."

I spent ages searching upstairs before I eventually found it under a cushion in the living room. She had been playing me all along. Instead of dismissing it for what it was, a simple childhood prank, I worried she was becoming manipulative and dishonest, like Nigel. I told myself his genes were taking over us both.

Mostly, I loved being a mum. But there were times when I felt trapped in a vortex of my own emotions. Physically, I had escaped the flat in Essex. But in many ways, I was still stuck there, and I wondered if that would always be so.

27

ONE AFTERNOON, Mum called and she was so upset she could hardly get her words out.

"I was shopping in Iceland, and I saw him," she gulped. "I saw Nigel Taylor. He's back in Oldham, Stace."

I was at once aghast, yet completely unsurprised. I had been expecting this, ever since he was released. I had driven myself mad with possibilities for so long that it was an odd sort of relief to hear my worst fears verbalised. I called the police, but they explained Nigel had not breached the restraining order simply by shopping in Oldham.

There was nothing they could do. Previously, I had been over-protective of Kadie, but now I went into over-drive. She was not allowed to play out with her friends. There were no sleepovers, no parties, no playdates, unless they were at our house. I had to supervise her at all times.

"Muuum," she moaned, when I said no to yet another party invite. "You're so strict."

"I know," I said gently. "And I'm sorry, Kades. I'm just trying to look after you."

But of course, she didn't understand, and she huffed out of the room and slammed the door. The problem with my boundaries was that they were artificial, they had not grown alongside me, through my own childhood. I had put them in place, ready-made and rigid, and so did not know how to bend or readjust them when needed. Not long afterwards, a neighbour told me he had seen Nigel hanging around the garages that backed onto our street.

"Nice that he's back," he commented. "I haven't seen him for ages."

He, like most people in Oldham, had no idea what Nigel had done or that he had been in prison. The court case had been reported in Essex, not in the Northwest, and I had confided in nobody beyond Mum and a couple of close friends. And so my local community was not aware of the danger he posed. Reeling, I mumbled something in reply and went inside to call the police.

"Is there any CCTV?" they asked. "Can you prove it?"

When I checked the garages, there were no cameras and so I had no evidence. My heart was in my mouth, waiting for the next sighting, waiting for the next move.

I will kill you and I will kill the baby.

I am always one step ahead of you Lou-Lou.

My fear was so palpable I could strum it, like a guitar string. I could see it too, shiny and tight, stretched across my eyeline. In the end, I moved house to another area of Oldham. But it was, I knew, only a delaying tactic. He would find us eventually, I was sure of it. And even on a new street, I did not let Kadie go anywhere without me. One Saturday morning,

I caught her climbing out of the living room window when she thought I was still in bed.

"I just want to play out with my mates," she complained. "I'm like a prisoner in this house."

With a whoosh, I was back to being 17, trapped in the flat in Essex.

"I would never keep you prisoner," I told her tearfully. "That's not what this is about."

But everything I did was marbled with fear. Worse, I could see it was spreading, like a virus, to Kadie, too. We lived in a purgatorial limbo. I was always waiting for Nigel to turn up and kill us. Before her move to high school, in September 2019, I was called in to see the safeguarding team.

"We'd like to arrange a support package for Kadie, including counselling," they told me. "We need you to tell her the truth. Tell her who her father is, and so she can start high school without any secrets."

Stunned, I could only shake my head in disbelief. Walking out of the meeting, I felt completely alone and cut adrift. I might as well have been dropped into the Indian Ocean and told to swim back to Oldham.

I had no idea at all how to broach the issue with Kadie in a way that was appropriate to her age and the circumstances. I didn't feel I was ready. I didn't think she was ready either. I felt under so much pressure.

Despite my distrust of social services, I called and asked for help, but a social worker said, "We don't have anyone else like you, Stace, on our records. You're a guinea pig in many respects. But you mustn't feel pushed into telling Kadie who her father is. Do it when you're ready."

I put the phone down feeling lonelier than ever. I understand the reasons for anonymity for victims of sexual offences. But for me, it has been a double-edged sword. Because of the anonymity and the silence surrounding the offences, nobody knew about them. The support services that existed to help me did not know about me, and I did not know about them. And because I could not speak out and share my problem, I was made to feel ashamed. I was hidden away behind closed doors like a dirty rag, a bad smell, a shameful secret. And when I needed help, it simply was not there. I would always advocate privacy and sensitivity surrounding sexual offences, but I think it's equally important that victims have a voice. Silence breeds shame.

And so those summer holidays, before Kadie started high school, were horrendous. Day by day, the pressure of my secret weighed heavier and heavier. As July rolled into August, my angst became full-blown panic. I couldn't look at Kadie without bursting into tears, knowing that to break my silence I must also break her heart.

"What's up, Mum?" she asked.

But I just shrugged and avoided her gaze. I am ashamed to say, for those last couple of weeks of the holidays, I shut myself away in my bedroom. I could not face her.

Her first day at school dawned and still, I had not told her. My pride at seeing her in her new uniform was completely eclipsed by my anxiety. But, at my next meeting with the school, it turned out that there was a long waiting list for counselling and there was no package in place to support Kadie. Had I told her the truth, she would have been left to cope alone, just as I was. It was fortunate, then, that I hadn't confided in her. But deep down, I knew I could not keep putting it off forever. I had been lied to all through my childhood, and here I was lying to Kadie. I hated those parallels. Like me, she had a right to know who her father was, no matter how painful the truth.

* * * *

The following summer, I was busy cooking tuna pasta when I realised I had run out of mayonnaise. Normally, I didn't like Kadie going out anywhere on her own, but there was a small corner shop on our street just a short walk away.

"Kades, be a love and get some mayo from the shop," I said to her.

As she left, I glanced out of the kitchen window and noticed a van which revved loudly before driving off at speed. I thought nothing of it. But when Kadie was not back 10 minutes later, I went to the front door. I spotted her further down the street, her shoulders shaking with sobs. Kadie rarely cried, she was just not the sort to make a fuss, and instantly I panicked.

"What's happened?" I called, rushing to meet her.

"I was followed by a van," she gasped. "Right down the street. I had to keep running. I didn't know what to do."

My heart stuttered.

"Did you get a look at who was inside?" I asked.

"Yeah," she shuddered. "It was a man with dark eyes. He looked so evil."

Fear swept over my skin in an icy blast. Ushering her into the house, I said, "I think you should stay indoors from now on, just to be on the safe side."

I called the police, but I had no concrete evidence of who was driving the van. Kadie and I went to stay with a friend, in South Yorkshire, for a few days. While we were away, Mum knocked on our neighbours' doors, requesting footage. She found several clips of the van tearing down the street, but the registration was partially obscured, and the police were not able to trace it.

"If anything else happens, let us know," they said.

We would never know for sure who was driving the van. But I was now certain of one thing, for her own safety, I had to tell Kadie the truth.

One night, as we watched TV, I brought up the subject of her father.

"You always say I don't have one," she said.

"I know," I winced. "But that isn't true, and the thing is, Kades, your dad is my dad. I don't know how else to say it. I am so sorry."

I explained, as sensitively as I could, how she had been created. I braced myself for a barrage of questions, but Kadie simply said, "Ok," and went back to watching television. Her reaction blindsided me. I worried it was too much for her to cope with, too momentous for her to take in. I wished, desperately, that I had support or advice in place, for me and for her.

A few weeks later, Kadie came into the bathroom while I was brushing my teeth, and said, "Does this mean you're my sister?"

"No," I said firmly. "I am your mother. I gave birth to you. I know it's a difficult situation but there should be no doubt in your mind. I am your mum and I love you so much."

She took a few days to digest this and then she said, "I want to meet Nigel Taylor. I want to know who I am."

My insides liquefied with pure terror.

"No!" I yelled, and then, more reasonably, "No, sorry, it's just not safe. He is a dangerous man."

Kadie shrugged with all the nonchalance of a 12-year-old.

"I get that," she said. "But I need to find that out for myself. He is my biological father."

I felt as though I had been sliced in two. Part of me understood just how she felt, aged seven, I had been enticed into meeting Nigel at the park. Like Kadie, I had wanted to know my family history. I understood the importance of having an identity. But as a mother, I could not even consider letting her meet him. I was in no doubt that Nigel would ruin Kadie, as he had ruined me. Again, the little ironies of my life were laid bare and raw.

"Look, let me talk to social services," I said. "We'll take their advice."

To my horror, the case worker said, "Maybe we could arrange a one-off meeting with Nigel and Kadie, under supervision."

As she spoke, I heard Nigel, screaming in my ear: *I will kill you, I will kill the baby.*

There was no way I could agree to them meeting, under any circumstance. Not only was Nigel a violent sex offender, but he was also manipulative and devious. I remembered the way he had persuaded me to go to the shop for sweets, the manner in which he had talked me into visiting him in Essex. He was almost more deadly below the surface. I could not let my daughter fall prey to that same process of coercion. But then the social worker said, "The problem is, after one meeting, Kadie might want to see him again. She might start contacting him. It might not be a good idea after all. The problem is, Stace, we don't know anyone else in your position. It's so hard to advise you."

Nobody really knew. Nobody could really help us.

Kadie and I were at loggerheads. She insisting she had every right to meet her father, me trying and failing to convince her of the dangers.

"You don't let me see my friends, you don't even let me see my own father!" she shouted. "You just don't want me to be happy."

I hated it when we argued and, as the weeks passed, I fell into a deep depression. A few months earlier, I'd lost my maternal grandparents, Ken and Joan, and I missed them so much. Grandad had died just days before his 80th birthday, from heart failure. Gran passed away 11 days later from a broken heart. I missed them both terribly.

Clouding my sadness for my grandparents was the dark and bitter pain of mourning people who were still alive. Losing my elderly grandparents was sad, but also expected. Losing my foster family was a wrench I would never come to terms with. And parallel to my sadness and grief, I worried, most of all, about Kadie. What kind of mother was I if I couldn't keep my child safe? My anxiety was so acute it manifested physically, and I was taken into hospital with stomach pains.

After tests, I was diagnosed with stress-induced ulcerative colitis. Some days, the pain was so bad, I needed a wheelchair to get around. After I was discharged, Kadie looked after me. Nothing was too much trouble for her, she had such a kind heart and a gentle nature. She deserved a loving family around her, was it too much to ask?

Slowly, we tried to work through our differences. It helped, too, that she was so close to Mum. Though I was grateful for that, my resentment towards Mum still simmered. All of my problems could be traced, like a trail of breadcrumbs, back to my childhood. Over Christmas 2020, the relationship between Mum and I was strained. After one minor argument, she got up to walk out, and I snapped, "Walk away from me! It wouldn't be the first time, would it?"

My anger crackled and hissed like an angry snake trapped inside me. On New Year's Eve, I came to a decision. For Kadie's sake, Mum and I needed to reconcile as many of our differences as we could. While the rest of the world prepared to celebrate the arrival of a New Year, Mum and I had a huge humdinger of a row. In many ways, it was like a clear-out, throwing up all the accusations and injustices that had festered for many years in the back rooms of my mind. Afterwards, I felt so much better, as though a fresh wind had blown right through the dusty cobwebs from the past. Finding my voice had done me good, and that evening, an embryonic idea began to take shape. The next morning, feeling alive and energised, I began to write.

"I'm going to write a blog," I told Mum. "Starting with my childhood, right up until today, I want to tell my story. If speaking out helps me, it might just help others as well."

28

OPENING MY social media, I posted the first chapter of 'The Life of Stace Don' on January 1, 2021, with the opening words:

At 2 years old everything started to go downhill… At that point, I suffered from bite marks, bruises and a broken leg. It wasn't clear who exactly was responsible, but I went into care, where I was brought up by a foster family. Everything appeared to be okay, but appearances can be deceiving…

As a young child in care, I always felt my childhood was pretty normal. A mum, a dad, siblings and friends. This was, however, not the happy ending I hoped it would be. At 10 years old it was all taken away from me and I was about to end up in a world many worlds apart from what I was used to. So not only was I removed from all I knew, but I was prevented from seeing the people who brought me up and I no longer had that feeling of safety and stability I had when I was with them. I began to suffer physical abuse. I was being hit with hands, a belt, I was made to eat a cigarette and I had nowhere to turn to. I was estranged and isolated, then I was kicked out of the house. And so at 13, I was moved to yet another place. I had to drop out of school and my ribs were broken and I had bruises all over me. I moved back to my mum for a short while then was kicked out another time. I lived on the streets and then was forced by circumstances to go back to my mum's again. I didn't feel I fit in or belonged, and it just became a very difficult time. I turned into a very angry child. I became someone I personally didn't even like myself. So I didn't have many friends, became very isolated and was bullied most of the way through because of how I was dressed and looked. I had gone from being well dressed, healthy and looked after, to a withdrawn, angry child and very underweight. I became bulimic, probably to feel a bit of control, as I couldn't understand my surroundings anymore and thought everyone hated me. I ended up hating myself. After being moved around a lot and being unsettled with no stability at 16 years old, I took an overdose. I genuinely didn't want to live anymore. This is my past in a nutshell. My story of what went on during my time as a child and a teenager. There is more to it, and I will talk about these events in more details at a later stage...

I closed the page and went off to bed with no expectations. The next day, my phone buzzed with notifications.

I can relate exactly to what you're saying.
You've inspired me with your honesty.
Where is Chapter 2? We can't wait!

I felt so humbled. After reading all the feedback, I unpacked my old trophies and my certificates, and remembered, with misty eyes, the journey we'd been on together.

You will make something of yourself, Stace. Your life will have purpose.

Perhaps then, my purpose in life was to be a mother and to share my trauma for the benefit of others.

Over the next few months, I gathered support from all around the world. One morning, I woke up to find I had over a thousand new followers in the US. I received messages from right across Europe, and as far away as Australia. I progressed from writing on social media to having my own website and I posted on Linktree, too.

Each time I wrote, I shared a different chapter of my life. Kadie was too young to be included in my story, but in every other way, I tried to be as honest and transparent as possible. Sometimes, my focus was emotional and psychological, looking at how to cope with those feelings of loneliness, shame and despair.

Other times, I concentrated on practical issues, how to navigate the court system, how to access counselling services, how to approach the issue of the right to anonymity. The response, every time, was beyond anything I could have dreamed of. Some people wanted advice about social services. Others asked for a step-by-step walk through of the police interview process for victims. Several people told me

I had given them the courage to report their abuse to the police. One, with mental health issues, said I had saved her life.

"I read your blog and realised I needed to speak out," she said. "I got help, and it saved me."

For me, that was everything. At last, I had direction and ambition. I felt useful and worthwhile. I was reminded of the time I had stepped off the coach in Oldham after leaving Essex, out of one life and into another. Starting my blog was, again, like the start of a whole new world.

And though I had intended to help others with my writing, I was helping myself too. I had messages from Maggie Oliver, who runs a foundation supporting survivors of CSE (child sexual exploitation), commending my work. She gave me lots of support. I was even invited to attend a charity call, run by the foundation. But the thought of dressing up in a ball gown was terrifying.

Ever since my time in Essex, I'd worn nothing but tracksuits. For me, it wasn't about clothing. It was about feeling safe. One environment where tracksuits were, thankfully, welcome, was the football field and I began playing football again. I joined a local team, I went to the gym and got myself fit. I studied health and social care at college, and I also volunteered at a local youth centre.

Best of all, my relationship with Kadie got better and better. She still wanted to meet Nigel, but she now accepted it was not a good idea.

"I'm proud of you, Mum," she smiled.

"Proud of you, too," I beamed.

I had been chatting, over those months, to a friend, Keran, who was two years older than me. It had started with me complaining about my wild hair on Snapchat and she had commented and offered some advice. It turned out we had lots in common and I knew she fancied me. I felt the same about her, but I could not allow myself to trust someone enough to fall in love. That part of me was damaged irreparably.

"I really like Keran," Kadie told me. "I don't mind if you go out with her. I think you'd be good together."

"We'll just stay friends for now," I told her. "I don't want to complicate things."

I could never quite seal the lid on my relationship with my foster family, so I contacted Donna and asked if she could arrange a meeting with my foster mother. We agreed to have coffee and, right up to the day itself, I was determined to be laid-back and self-assured. I reminded myself not to rake over the past, not to dredge up the heartbreak from my childhood. But the moment I saw her, it all came tumbling out, a landslide of emotions, one falling over the next.

"I never wanted to leave," I said to her. "That was my home, with you. I was safe there. You know, I never felt safe again afterwards. I really wanted to come home, for years and years."

She did not speak, but she took my hand in hers. And then, it was time for her to leave. Afterwards, I felt empty and unfulfilled, as though I had bared my soul and got nothing in return. I was angry with myself for wasting my chance with her. A few months later, I messaged to ask if we could meet up again. This time, I was planning a completely new approach. Instead of scraping over old wounds, I had decided to focus solely on the present.

"I'm doing really well at college," I announced. "I'm hoping to get a good job when I graduate. And Kadie's doing brilliantly at school. Everything has worked out so well. You should come and see our new house, it's lovely. I decorated it all myself."

I was doing it again. Over-selling myself, creating a perfect life that simply did not exist. Even now, I was trying to impress her. I was trying to be the kind of person I thought she wanted me to be, the kind of person who would be welcome in her life. Again, I felt crushed when we said goodbye. For months afterwards, I heard nothing. I messaged once or twice, suggesting we could meet up. But there was no reply. In the end, in tears, I typed out:

Was it me? Was I just not good enough?

Again, there was no response, and I accepted that was the end. But even now, aged 36, I would jump at the chance to meet up with my foster parents for a cheesy pizza and a game of Scrabble. A part of me is, and always will be, seven years old, wrapped up in the warmth and love of their household. That was the last time I truly felt safe. After the first meeting with Nigel in the park, a hairline crack had appeared at my core. And the more I saw him, the more I cracked. There were many times I feared I might be irreparable.

I understand the Robinsons coped with their own loss after I left, and I do not know what they went through. I only hope all foster carers understand that fostering is a long-term commitment. Children have hearts and souls. They cannot be picked up and dropped again and again. If you drop them repeatedly, they will break.

29

EARLY IN 2022, Keran travelled from her home in Northern Ireland to visit. We had such a wonderful time and by the end of it, we were officially in a relationship.

"Told you!" Kadie beamed. "I knew you'd be a good match."

Keran and I were great for each other, she was down to earth and practical, and she had a heart of gold. As we got serious, and with Kadie's permission, I confided in her about Nigel. Keran was understandably shocked and emotional, but afterwards, she treated me no differently, and I loved her for that.

Late in 2022, me and Kadie made the decision to move to Northern Ireland. Part of me was still running away from the past. But I was also running towards a brighter future. Keran proposed at the end of the year and our wedding is booked for the summer of 2025. I never dreamed I'd find love like this, and I feel so incredibly lucky. Better still, I can finally give Kadie the family I'd always dreamed of. We've picked out a wedding venue and booked the registrar and I would really like to be able to wear a wedding dress, even if only for the ceremony. But I worry my anxiety will spin out of control without my trusted tracksuit to keep me calm. Keran has insisted I will look just as lovely in a white tracksuit and who knows, maybe I can set a trend!

The scars of my past run deep. This is a journey fraught with hurdles and there is no magic cure. I struggle to eat out in public, I become irrationally panicky if I can't find a simple meal on a menu. Just last week I burst into tears and had to leave a restaurant. I felt embarrassed – inside I am still that little girl, forced to sit at the table in the dark on my own and eat until I am physically sick.

I have legally removed my middle name, Louise. Nigel was the only one who called me 'Lou-Lou' and I cannot bear to hear it. Because of the tight shoes I wore through high school, I have lasting damage to my feet. My two middle toes overlap, and I wear a spacer to keep them apart. I've been advised I need surgery, but I can't face the thought of being stuck on the football side-lines while I recover. I play for a local team in Northern Ireland and I'm as competitive and passionate as ever. I've been so pleased at the growth of women's football over the past couple of years and I hope it continues. The sport carried me through the darkest and toughest times of my childhood and I know it can do the same for other girls.

Despite the bad memories in Essex, I support Southend FC. In 2006, they beat Manchester United 1-0 and I love that David beat Goliath on that day. I will always root for the underdog. Perhaps a part of me just cannot completely move on from the attacks in Essex, I am bonded to the trauma. As much as I want to let it go, I hang onto it, too. For although it was the worst time of my life, it was also the best– because it was where my daughter's life began. Southend was where the miracle started.

Mum and I are closer now, and she has a wonderful relationship with Kadie. I can forgive the small splinters of unhappiness from my childhood, the too-tight shoes, the fraught mealtimes, the emotional distance. But there are big boulders of suffering too, packing me off to live with Nigel, not stopping me from going to Essex that Christmas, refusing to pick me up from Essex after he ripped up my coach ticket. These are events that changed – and almost ended – my life. Maybe I can't forgive, but I can accept, and I can move on.

What happened to me was not primarily Mum's fault at all, but I wish she could have been there for me. I can't change the past, but happily, she is there for me now. She came to visit recently to see our wedding venue and any time I'm stressed or upset, she jumps on a flight to come and comfort me. I have a greater understanding now of what Mum went through too. As a parent myself, I know it's not always easy. As mums, we just have to keep on trying. Society expects a lot from mothers. More than that, we expect a lot of ourselves, maybe we expect too much, and so often we build ourselves up to fail. I'm always telling my blog followers to be kind to themselves, but I find it hard to follow my own advice.

My blog now has tens of thousands of followers from over 50 countries, as far away as the US and Australia and including the UK, Turkey, Ireland, Spain, Vietnam, Canada and Hungary. I have 11k followers in the US alone. Writing my blog has finally freed me of the cancer of shame which had eaten away at me for so long. I've still got my old trophies and certificates in my bedroom, and I still have the battered old football that I carried with me on my miserable journey. Even on the darkest days, those trophies kept that glimmer of hope flickering within me.

One day you will make something of your life.

I didn't choose this path, it chose me, but I hope I can use my blog to move forward in my career. I'm a survivor learning to live, and I want to help others to learn to live too. I would like to work with disadvantaged children, supporting them through trauma, and being that person that as a child, I never had.

The interview process for any job is a huge hurdle, I can't turn up for a role as a youth support worker in a tracksuit. Yet neither can I bear to wear a smart suit. I wish employers could look beyond my clothes and see me for the person I am, a committed and loyal advocate for children in need. I'm also planning to train as a football coach, which is one place where my tracksuit will be welcome!

I feel proud to have turned my trauma into a positive force, the very thing which threatened to ruin me is now helping me and helping others. My weakness has become my strength, and my story has given me power. Best of all, my story brought my beautiful daughter into the world.

These days, I am honest with Kadie. We have no more secrets, no more lies. I am trying, slowly, to give her some freedom, to make up for the early years when I barely let her out of my sight. She's studying for her GCSEs, and hopes to become a mental health nurse, speaking both English and Spanish. We enjoy bowling and going to the cinema and like most teenagers, she loves a cheeky Nando's. Recently, Kadie went away to her pal's caravan without me, which was as necessary as it was nerve-racking. I understand we can't spend our lives in hiding and I don't want that for Kadie. But it pulls at my heartstrings, every time she walks out of the door.

For her 16th birthday, I bought her a helicopter ride because, quite literally, I am trying to give her wings to fly. 'My Girl' is a book for both of us, the little girl I was never allowed to be and the wonderful girl my daughter is. I could not be prouder of you.

Love you, Kades.

A Letter from Kadie

WHEN I was younger, I wondered who and where my dad was, but Mum was constantly pushing my questions away for reasons I never understood. I thought she was hiding him from me and it wasn't until I got older, I realised it wasn't at all what I'd thought.

I didn't understand why she was so strict, it seemed she just made rules up for the sake of it. I was hardly allowed out of the house and constantly having to cancel my plans with friends, because they didn't include her. I even thought for years maybe she didn't want me to have any friends or a life away from her. It was only after she explained who my father was that I started to understand why she was so protective. Still, I wanted to meet him, to make up my own mind. Not because I didn't believe her, but because I needed to see him for myself. I was confused and the curiosity got the better of me and I wanted answers. I didn't feel I could ask Mum because it was so upsetting for us both. It took a while for me to see that Mum does her best for me, and if she says it's not a good idea, I can accept that.

I don't really discuss my situation with anyone, it's not something I find easy to talk about. But at the same time, I am really proud of Mum for doing her book and managing to speak out about it, and I want to support her in every way I possibly can. To other young people like me, I'd say that really, you don't need a dad. I've been really unlucky with my dad, but I've been more than lucky with my mum, and maybe it all balances out.

Despite the situation I wouldn't change my family for the world, it might not be a typical family, but it's my family, and that's what matters.

Love you, Mum.

A Letter from Lisa

I HAVE always loved my daughter from the moment she was born, my first child, my little princess. When she was younger, I thought I was doing my best to look after her, but I know now I let her down a lot, and I'm really sorry about that.

I'm not making excuses, but I had an unhappy childhood, As an adult I chose the wrong relationships, always trying to make everyone else happy at my own cost – and Stace's cost too. I felt vulnerable and I couldn't stand up for myself. My world fell apart completely when I lost a child. All was going well in my pregnancy up to 36 weeks when a scan showed there was no heartbeat. I had to deliver my son naturally and I thought I was going to die giving birth that night. I was so numb.

I always felt I was fighting everything and everyone alone. The more I did, the more it went wrong I tried so hard, but up until recently I didn't truly understand what was so wrong with everything I did. I can't change the things that have happened, but I have definitely taken back control of my life after being controlled by the wrong people for so long.

I want to focus on the future now, and I have built a great relationship with my daughter and have the most amazing bond with my granddaughter. I love them with my every breath and could not be prouder of everything Stace has done in her adult life. I am so sorry for what she went through as a child, it breaks my heart to think of how she suffered on her own.

She is and always will be my inspiration.

Acknowledgements

MY DAUGHTER for growing up to be the kindest caring person. My mum for changing her life around and being the best ninny to Kadie. My nana and grandad although not here still give me strength.

My fiancée for showing me what love is and how to love and giving me and Kadie the family we longed for. My best friend for showing me normality! And allowing me to be godmother to the most beautiful children.

Jasper for being the best editor for my blog. Ann for giving me this opportunity, without you this wouldn't be possible. Cathy my family therapist for being our constant support and understanding me.

Finally, every single one of my followers; I honestly wouldn't be where I am today if it wasn't for your support and kindness, you're the extended family I never knew we needed.

www.thelifeofstacedon.wordpress.com

Other bestselling Mirror Books written by Ann Cusack